Stepping Closer to the Savior

Melanie M. Redd

CROSSBOOKS
PUBLISHING

CrossBooks™
A Division of LifeWay
1663 Liberty Drive
Bloomington, IN 47403
www.crossbooks.com
Phone: 1-866-879-0502

First published by CrossBooks 6/1/2010

ISBN: 978-1-6150-7138-8 (sc)

Library of Congress Control Number: 2010922082

Printed in the United States of America
Bloomington, Indiana

This book is printed on acid-free paper.

Contents

How to Begin a Relationship with Jesus Christ

To start a relationship with Jesus, you simply need to know your A, B, C's.

The "A" in the A, B, and C's is to <u>Admit</u> you are a sinner, and in need of salvation from sin. All of us have made mistakes, and we need a Savior. Romans 3:10 tells us, *"As it is written: There is no one righteous, not even one."* (NIV) And Romans 3:23 reiterates, *"For all have sinned and fall short of the glory of God."* (NIV) Even the most kind and considerate person on this earth is a sinner in need of a Savior.

> A= Admit you are a sinner.
>
> B= Believe that Jesus Christ is the Son of God.
>
> C= Confess your sin to Jesus.

As an eleven year old girl, I realized I was a sinner heading straight to hell. I prayed and told God that I knew I needed a Savior. To personally know Jesus, you will need to pray also.

The "B" in the A, B, C's is to <u>Believe</u> that Jesus Christ is the Son of God, and that He is the only way to obtain salvation – to get to heaven. The Bible tells us in John 14:6, *"Jesus answered, 'I am the way and the truth and the life. No one comes to the Father except through Me.'"* (NIV) To enter a relationship with God, we must trust in His Son, Jesus Christ, and believe that He alone can save us.

> "Dear God, I know that I am a sinner. I'm sorry for my sin. Take my sin away. Forgive me of my sin. Thank you for forgiving me. Jesus, come into my heart and life. Thank you for coming in. I give my life to you. Thank you for saving me. Amen."

The "C" in the A, B, and C's is to <u>Confess</u> your sin. This means to admit your sin. 1 John 1:9 tells us, *"If we confess our sins, He is faithful and just and will forgive us our sins and purify us from all unrighteousness."* (NIV) Confession is agreeing with God that we are not perfect and inviting Him to forgive us for all that is impure and imperfect in our lives.

Not only must we confess Jesus privately, we must also confess Him publicly. With our mouths, we need to tell someone that we are trusting in Jesus to save us. Romans 10:9-10 simply states, *"That if you confess with your mouth, 'Jesus is Lord,' and believe in your heart that God raised him from the dead, you will be saved. For it is with your heart that you believe and are justified, and it is with your mouth that you confess and are saved."* (NIV)

If you have never done so, you can receive Jesus today. To receive Jesus, to obtain salvation, you can pray something like this…

"Dear God, I know that I am a sinner. I'm sorry for my sin. Take my sin away. Forgive me of my sin. Thank you for forgiving me. Jesus, come into my heart and life. Thank you for coming in. I give my life to you. Thank you for saving me. Amen."

If you have prayed this prayer today and invited Jesus into your life, let someone know! Tell a trusted friend, pastor, or teacher about your decision. These friends will be so glad to hear what has happened, and they will be able to pray with you about your decision. You have made the best decision today that you could ever make!

Tea Cups – Fragile or Useful?

A few years ago, our family moved to a new church where my husband served as one of the pastors. We began to meet people and get involved in their lives. So many people would come up to us and ask us questions like: *"How do I have a personal time alone with God? How do I develop a better prayer life? How can I share my faith with my neighbor?"*

As we heard these questions, we would often type long emails to them or meet them for lunch to explain in-depth answers to their questions. Sometimes we would suggest a good book or a Bible study to these folks. However, we could not find a practical resource that we could put in their hands to help them better succeed in the Christian life. I looked online and all over bookstores for a simple resource that we could share with our friends, but I did not find one that answered basic questions.

So, my sweet husband suggested that I write and compile such a resource, putting into a book all of those things I'd been sharing over lunch, teaching in Bible studies, and emailing to people for years. I took the information and compiled it into seven sections.

Each of these sections is just a basic part of the Christian life that many believers learned growing up in the church. However, the longer we have served in ministry, the more we see that many adults did not grow up in strong churches. Many adult believers were never taught some of the basics of the Christian walk. No one showed them the most important and crucial practices of the faith.

That is what this book is about – basic steps we each can and must take to grow closer to our Savior. Each step is meant to increase our faith and to daily draw us closer to Jesus.

First, this book explains the "why" of the basics of the Christian life. Why should we have a quiet time? Why should we pray? What difference does it make that we meditate on God's Word? This book lays out the rationale for stepping closer to the Savior.

Then, you are given the chance to "try out" each of these steps for yourself. You will be presented with activities and exercises that will allow you the opportunity to personally try each step. Hopefully, as each step is practiced, it will become a part of your life, integral to your daily routine.

As one of my friends "tried out" these steps for herself, she began to have a daily quiet time for the first time in her life. She began to grow closer to Jesus and to desire a more intimate relationship with Him. There is joy and peace now in her life that she has never known before. All she needed was something or someone to show her how to "do" the Christian life.

> "Draw near to God, and He will draw near to you."
> James 4:8 (NASB)

The Bible encourages us in James 4:8, *"Draw near to God, and He will draw near to you."* (NASB) This book is all about drawing close to God and inviting

Him to draw close to us. You will be encouraged to take steps each day that will draw you closer to the Savior.

One of my grandmothers was a collector of tea cups. I have inherited many of those beautiful old porcelain cups and saucers. However, most days these lovely containers perch empty on a cabinet shelf in my home. They don't get used at all. The tea cups exist to decorate my home and to remember my sweet grandmother.

> **May we be useful vessels and not just fragile china "cups" perched on a shelf!**

They were made, however, to be used for drinking coffee or hot tea. At one time, these cups were filled to the brim with hot tea and served to guests in my grandmother's home. Many people enjoyed the refreshment provided in these floral cups. My antique cups were once incredibly useful, but now just sit empty and serve only for décor.

Similarly, many Christians are like my tea cups. They are beautiful on the outside and could offer such refreshment to others around them. However, they sit empty and useless on the church pews because they have not been filling up with the Lord Jesus Christ. They have so much potential, but they are empty and useless.

To make my tea cups useful again, all I need to do is fill them once again with coffee or tea. And, all that most Christians need to do to be useful again is to start spending daily time alone with God, asking Him to fill them up with Himself. Once full, you and I can be used by the Lord to encourage and to refresh others around us.

I pray that you will be filled up with Jesus as you take steps closer to Him in this study. May we be useful vessels and not just fragile china "cups" perched on a shelf!

Blessings to you,

Melanie Redd

Helpful Hints in Getting Started

1. Don't do this study by yourself.

You may choose to use this resource to help someone else to step closer to Jesus. There may be people in your sphere of influence who need a guide and a practical plan for growing in their faith. They may not know how to start or what to do. Use this resource to assist them.

> **Don't do this study by yourself.**

2. Make sure you have a great Bible to use.

We also want to encourage you to use a Bible that is easy to read and understand. If you are working with another person or a small group, make sure they also have good, readable Bibles to use for this study. In recent years, I have been using the New Living Translation for my own Bible reading. This translation is quite easy to read and to understand.

To help you in choosing, why not visit a local Christian bookstore. Pull Bibles of different translations from the shelves and look through them. Read the same verse in each translation and see which is easiest for you to grasp. (It's okay to sit on the floor and do this!) Flip through to see what additional resources the Bibles offer as well – index, concordance, study helps, etc.

> **Make sure you have a great Bible to use.**

3. **Don't quit!**

Don't quit!

If you miss a day, start up again the following day. This is not a sprint to the finish line, but rather a slow, steady walk down a long road. We've set up this study to start simply and encourage you to get moving toward the Savior. You will seek to get to know Him a little better each day for the next seven weeks. Then, we pray, you will continue to pursue your love relationship with Him for the rest of your life.

Why Do I Need to Step Closer to Jesus?

a few years ago, my husband, an avid golfer, invited me to learn to play golf. He thought golf would be a great sport for us to play together. On our first outing, we rented some clubs, and he showed me the basics. I learned to hold the clubs correctly and how to stand and swing. Then, he taught me the rule that he suggested was the "key" rule for all of golf. When I follow this one rule, I play well, but, if I mess up on this one thing, my whole game suffers.

I must – at all times – keep my head down with my eye on the ball as I swing the golf club. It seems simple, but most golfers like to look up and see how far they hit the ball. Often, especially with new golfers, they look up from the ball too quickly and hit poorly. I have done this many times, especially when I first started to play.

However, once I learned to focus intently on the golf ball with my head down, I actually was able to hit the ball well. Instead of dribbling down the fairway a few feet, my ball actually began to fly through the air.

In our spiritual lives, there is also one "key" to success. This key practice leads us to grow closer to the Lord and stay close to Him. I believe this one practice is at the heart of my Christian walk both as a new Christian and now after over 30 years of walking with Him. When I practice this spiritual step, life is just better. However, when I neglect this step or skip this step – I get into all kinds of messes.

What is this "key" or main step that we should take to know God better? It's simply to spend personal time alone with Him daily! Time alone with my Savior is the most important and essential thing that I do all day long! It's the launching pad to all other practices and disciplines in the Christian life.

> Time alone with my Savior is the most important and essential thing that I do all day long! It's the launching pad to all other practices and disciplines in the Christian life.

There is nothing we can do each morning more important than to take a few moments and focus on the Lord. When we lift up our eyes to the Creator of this universe, we are changed. When we open God's Word each morning, we are given directions, wisdom, help, and encouragement for the day.

Psalm 121:1 states it this way, *"I lift up my eyes to the hills; where does my help come from? My help comes from the Lord, the maker of heaven and earth."* (NIV)

<u>Think about this for a minute…</u>

- Where do you look for help?
- Do you get up in the morning and go to the Bible?
- Or, do you turn on one of the major news programs for your morning fill up?

> "I lift up my eyes to the hills; where does my help come from? My help comes from the Lord, the maker of heaven and earth."
> Psalm 121:1 (NIV)

The Psalmist encourages us in Psalm 121 to look up – to literally lift up our eyes and look up. In ancient days, the hills were associated with help. To be up high on the hill was to be safe and secure from predators and enemies. In fact, Jerusalem is uphill and high from every direction. Whether you are entering from the north, south, east, or west, you must go up to get to the city of Jerusalem.

Many of the altars in Biblical times were set up on hills on the roads to Jerusalem. These altars were erected to pagan gods. According to Jeremiah 3:23, *"Truly in vain is salvation hoped for from the hills, and from the multitude of mountains: truly in the LORD our God is the salvation of Israel."* (NKJV)

In Scripture, we are encouraged to look above the hills – go to the top! Go above the mountains to the One who made the hills and the mountains – the Lord Almighty!

According to Psalm 23:1, we are to remember that, *"The Lord is my Shepherd, I shall not want."* (NKJV) David's words ring out throughout the Psalms for us to look to the Lord for our shelter, our provision, our help, and our hope.

Isaiah reminds us to look to the Lord in Isaiah 40:26 where he tells us to *"Lift your eyes and look to the heavens: Who created all these? He who brings out the starry host one by one, and calls them each by name. Because of His great power and mighty strength, not one of them is missing."* (NIV)

> **"Lift your eyes and look to the heavens: Who created all these? He who brings out the starry host one by one, and calls them each by name. Because of His great power and mighty strength, not one of them is missing." Isaiah 40:26 (NIV)**

Again in Isaiah 51:6, we are admonished to, *"Look up to the skies above and gaze down on the earth beneath. For the skies will disappear like smoke, and the earth will wear out like a piece of clothing; the people of the earth will die like flies, but My salvation lasts forever. My righteous rule will never end!"* (NLT)

For several years, I taught third grade. I got to meet and instruct many wonderful kids over the years, and I found one particular habit to be consistent in every truly smart student that I taught: they looked up and they kept their eyes on me as often as they possibly could. The brightest students didn't want to miss anything; they stayed alert and attentive to what I was saying and doing as the teacher.

God is our Master Teacher and He wants us to be alert to Him – watching, listening, and aware of what He is doing. When we talk to Him, spend time in His Word, and even just sit quietly in His Presence, we become better students.

However, some of the children I taught who struggled the most were those who never looked up, never seemed to be listening, and rarely paid attention. If they had only looked my way from time to time, their perspective and their grades would have greatly improved. I tried everything I could to

3

engage them, but they just had other things vying for their attention.

We do the same thing to our heavenly Teacher, don't we? We look everywhere else but up and into His eyes for help. He calls us, He prods us, He encourages us, and He longs for us to look up. But, we have many other things vying for our attention.

> **He calls us, He prods us, He encourages us, and He begs us to look up. But, we have many other things vying for our attention.**

<u>Think about this for a minute…</u>

- Why should we look to Him?
- Why does it really matter?
- What distracts you and vies for your attention other than the Lord?

Let's take a moment to think about why we need to get up every day and lift our eyes up to our Savior. I have highlighted a few main reasons for us to look up to the Lord every morning, though there are many more. Let's consider why it matters that we personally meet with God each day.

> **God is our Helper.**

The first reason we are encouraged to look up is to <u>find help from our God</u>. <u>God is our Helper</u>. Psalm 121:2 states, *"My help comes from the LORD, who made the heavens and the earth!"* (NLT) *My help comes from Jehovah God, the self-subsisting God who needs no help. He is able to spend His energies and His time helping us!*

I love the words of David in Psalm 118:5-8, *"In my distress I prayed to the LORD and the LORD answered me and rescued me. The LORD is for me, so I will not be afraid. What can mere mortals do to me? Yes, the LORD is for me; He will help me. I will look in triumph at those who hate me. It is better to trust the LORD than to put confidence in people."* (NLT)

Years ago, when my children were very small, I was literally praying in my master bathroom closet. It was a large closet, and I would go there when I needed just a moment of peace and quiet. On that particular morning, I remember that my heart was heavy and I didn't know exactly how to pray for the things that were upsetting me.

While I was sitting there trying to decide what to say to God, my two year old daughter Emily came into the closet with me. She was in tears and very upset. She plopped down in my lap, looked up at me, and said, *"Help, Momma!"* That's all I needed to hear from her. My arms went around her; I held her and patted her a bit. Then, she dried her tears, got up, and left me there in the closet.

As I sat there in the stillness of that moment, I had this thought that I believe came from the Lord; *"Child, you can come to Me just like your child came to you. Climb up in My lap and ask Me for help."* And, in that moment, I looked up and mouthed the word, *"Help!"*

> "Child, you can come to Me just like your child came to you. Climb up in My lap and ask Me for help."

God is available and waiting for us to just look up and ask Him for help. He is there for you. Will you look up today and invite Him to help you with whatever is weighing on your heart and life?

There's a second reason to look up to the Lord. He is our Creator and Maker. In *The Message*, the passage reads: *"I look up to the mountains; does my strength come from mountains? No, my strength comes from God, who made heaven, and earth, and mountains."* Psalm 121:1-2 (MSG)

> He is our Creator & Maker. "I look up to the mountains; does my strength come from mountains? No, my strength comes from God, who made heaven, and earth, and mountains." Psalm 121:1-2 (MSG)

When God gets too "small" in my eyes and in my life, all I have to do is go outside and look around at His creation. Take me to see the mountains, the ocean, a lake, or some beautiful flowers, and I am reminded of how big my God really is. Let me notice a flock of birds flying overhead or drive me toward a gorgeous sunset and my world gains perspective once again.

Awhile back, my kids and I went outside on a cool, clear night to look at the stars. We bundled up in jackets and went to lie out on the top of our trampoline in the backyard. Our house was out in the country, and on a clear night, you could literally see thousands of stars.

We all three laid on our backs looking up into the sky. Stars were shooting across the black expanse. It was a beautiful night and an incredible sight to behold. While we were taking it all in, I just quietly said to the kids, *"God is really an amazing God, isn't He."*

> **"God is really an amazing God, isn't He."**

My children began to talk about how great God was as they looked out into His creation with wonder. We talked about how He just told those stars to stay in place, and they did. We spent almost an hour that night contemplating the great power and creativity of our Creator God.

Think about this for a minute…

- Do you ever look at creation and think about your great and amazing God?
- How does His creation make you want to spend time with Him?

> **"He is our Keeper. He will not suffer thy foot to be moved: He that keepeth thee will not slumber. Behold, He that keepeth Israel shall neither slumber nor sleep. The LORD is thy Keeper:" Psalm 121:3-5a (KJV)**

For me, I look up and into the eyes of my God because He's the One who is holding this universe and our planet together. The same God who is able to keep back the tides and hold the stars in place is the same God who loves you and me and cares about our lives. So, we look up and recognize Him as our Creator.

A third reason we look to God each day is that He is our Keeper. According to Psalm 121:3-5a, *"He will not suffer thy foot to be moved: He that keepeth thee will not slumber. Behold, He that keepeth Israel shall neither slumber nor sleep. The LORD is thy Keeper:"* (KJV)

One of my favorite songs is by a man named Phil Joel. The title of the song is simply, *"God is Watching Over You."* So many times this song has come on the radio or my iPOD on a day when I really needed to hear it. One of my favorite lines in the song encourages me when it states, *"God is watching over you, as always. You are loved whatever you go through. He's right beside you."* [1]

Our God doesn't doze, take a nap, fall asleep, or even "zone out" for a minute. He is alert and watchful 24/7. Over and over in the Bible, we are promised that He is with us – right in the midst of our best moments and our hardest moments.

According to Isaiah 43:2-3, *"When you go through deep waters and great trouble, I will be with you. When you go through rivers of difficulty, you will not drown! When you walk through the fire of oppression, you will not be burned up; the flames will not consume you. For I am the LORD, your God, the Holy One of Israel, your Savior."* (NLT)

Knowing He is with me, I go to Him each morning and look into His face because I never know what the day holds! I don't know what the next phone call, email, or knock on the door might mean. So, I know that I need to look up to Him.

A fourth reason that I look to the Lord each morning is that <u>He is our Protector</u>. In Psalm 121:5-8, we read, *"The LORD himself watches over you! The LORD stands beside you as your protective shade. The sun will not hurt you by day, nor the moon at night. The LORD keeps you from all evil and preserves your life. The LORD keeps watch over you as you come and go, both now and forever."* (NLT)

That phrase "watches over" comes from the word "shâmar" which literally means to hedge about (as with thorns), that is, guard; generally to protect, attend to. God promised to guard us, protect us, and to hedge us about.

We keep the most wonderful old throw blanket on the back of our couch. When it gets a little cool or we want to just snuggle up under something warm, we grab the old, comfy

> We increase our ability, stability, and responsibility when we increase our sense of accountability to God.

> "When you go through deep waters and great trouble, I will be with you. When you go through rivers of difficulty, you will not drown! When you walk through the fire of oppression, you will not be burned up; the flames will not consume you. For I am the LORD, your God, the Holy One of Israel, your Savior." Isaiah 43:2-3 (NLT)

blanket. There is something comforting about being warmed beneath the threads of that covering.

So also, we have a heavenly *"Comforter."* Our God is there every moment of every day to provide warmth and comfort and safety. He is our shade. He is our Help through the darkest night. He keeps us from all harm and protects us from evil. God watches over us as we come and as we go. He never stops watching or protecting us – even when we are unaware of His presence.

> "He is our Protector. "The LORD himself watches over you! The LORD stands beside you as your protective shade. The sun will not hurt you by day, nor the moon at night. The LORD keeps you from all evil and preserves your life. The LORD keeps watch over you as you come and go, both now and forever."
> Psalm 121:5-8 (NLT)

A famous story is told at Baylor University, my alma mater. I was told this story when I first arrived at college and to this day I don't know the girl's name or exactly when this event took place. However, I share it with you to encourage you that God is watching over us all the time.

A Baylor student was returning home from the library one night a little later than she had planned. At the time, the Baylor campus was extremely spread out and not very well-lit. As this girl walked quickly back to her dorm, she didn't see or talk to anyone else.

The next day, she was stopped by the campus police and asked about some men that had been harassing some female students the night before. She told the police that she was not aware of any events and that she had not encountered any men the night before as she walked back from the library.

The police informed her that some delinquents had seen her and planned to harm her, but then two large "dudes" had joined her and had walked her home. She assured the police that she had been alone for her entire journey back to the dorm. The police only explained that these two "dudes" who accompanied her home had saved her from harm.

On her way out of the campus police station, it occurred to the female student that God had stepped in and sent His protection the night before. He was watching over her and keeping her safe even when she was unaware of any danger. And, from that time forward, I never walked across that campus at night without praying for God to send my "dudes" to protect me as well.

Why do I look to Jesus each day? I look to Him because He is my Protector and because I know He is closely watching over me and looking out for my welfare.

Think about this for a minute...

- Have you ever thought about the idea that God is watching over you?
- What does it mean to you to know that He is looking out for you and protecting you?

> "He is our place of peace! Come to Me, all of you who are weary and carry heavy burdens, and I will give you rest." Matthew 11:28 (NLT)

One final reason I turn daily to look in the face of my God is because He is our Place of Peace! Jesus' own words encourage us in Matthew 11:28, *"Come to Me, all of you who are weary and carry heavy burdens, and I will give you rest."* (NLT)

Rest. I look to Him each morning because I need for my heart and mind and soul to be at rest – to be stilled and calmed as I enter my day. My world is wild and crazy, and daily I need to enter into the quiet place of rest and refreshment that God offers.

This rest is much like the deep recesses of the ocean. Most of us only see the waves and hear the roar and crash of the water. We watch the tides roll and pitch, and we observe boats tossing about on the water. But, deep beneath the surface is a place of quiet peace. If you go down far enough into the ocean's depths, even the roughest hurricane or typhoon can't disrupt the peace and quiet.

My constant prayer is that I will go to that place of deep quiet in my life so that even the roughest "hurricanes" won't disrupt my peace. As I get quiet and still before God, I ask Him to quiet my soul and to give me that calm place of rest that can't be disturbed by anything in the external world.

> I also realize that my God has absolute and total control of things!!

When I miss my time alone with the Lord, I miss the peace and the deep sense of calm in my heart. However, when I look up, I realize that I have absolutely NO control over my world. But, I also realize that my God has absolute and total control of things!!

Throughout this chapter, I've shared with you some of the reasons that I spend time daily alone with God. He is our Helper, our Creator, our Keeper, our Protector, and our Peace.

To sum up Chapter One:

We lift up our eyes to the Lord because...				
He is our Helper!	He is our Creator & Maker!	He is our Keeper!	He is our Protector!	He is our Place of Peace!

Moving forward from here...

> This week, why not try spending a few minutes each morning alone with the Lord – just you, your Bible, and God?

This week, why not try spending a few minutes each morning alone with the Lord – just you, your Bible, and God? There is so much to gain from getting quiet before Him and inviting Him to fill up your cup.

For assistance with this, continue on to the "Try It for Yourself" section on the next page. Week One will show you how to have a quiet time and give you five chances to try it for yourself. It's not hard at all. Why not give it a try?

STEP ONE: TIME ALONE WITH GOD

Step Closer to the Savior

Try it for yourself!

*O*ne of the first things that I learned as a disciple of the Lord Jesus was how to have a quiet time—how to spend personal time alone with the Savior. There are so many wonderful systems, methods, books, and helps related to this topic. And, I encourage you to check out the devotional section in your local Christian bookstore.

However, no matter how many wonderful resources are available, the greatest challenge most of us have is following through on time alone with God. We desire and hope to spend time with Him, but then we oversleep, get a phone call, have to deal with a family member, or something else happens, and we miss our time with Him. This first chapter is dedicated to encouraging you to get in the habit of spending at least a few moments alone with God every day.

> Would you like to begin spending more quality time alone with the Lord?

<u>This week's challenging questions</u> – Would you like to begin spending more quality time alone with the Lord? How might time alone with God make a positive impact on your life?

Day One – Look at our heavenly Role Model & Step Closer to Him

....

 Warm-Up and Stretch

As you begin this week's lesson, jot down your ideas in response to a couple of questions:

When you think of having a quiet time with God, what comes to mind?

_____

What picture comes to mind when you hear the word "devotion"?

_____

> **"Today, begin to show me the path of life. I want to experience fullness of joy by spending time in Your presence. Allow me to experience pleasures as I spend time at Your right hand. Thank You for meeting with me today."**
> **Psalm 16:11 (NKJV)**

Start your time alone with God by simply talking to God in prayer. Tell Him that you desire to get more spiritually fit. Read this adapted version of a verse as your prayer to the Lord, *"Today, begin to show me the path of life. I want to experience fullness of joy by spending time in Your presence. Allow me to experience pleasures as I spend time at Your right hand. Thank You for meeting with me today." Psalm 16:11 (NKJV)*

 Exercise Your Spiritual Muscles

In the following box make a list of the three most amazing and incredible people you've ever known or read about. These can include world leaders, religious leaders, preachers, athletes, scholars, or maybe even family members. Fill out the names, and then explain briefly why these people amaze and inspire you.

Amazing People:	Why they are amazing & inspiring to you:

Now, go back up and mark that one person who most amazes and inspires you. Why did you choose this person as your number one inspiration?

There are many outstanding and wonderful men and women that you could have listed. And, if we compared our lists, we might find some common ground. One person at the top of my list is the Lord Jesus Christ. There is so much about Him and His life that inspires and amazes me.

For this exercise, you will look at the God-man, Jesus. He was both fully God and fully man. His walk on this earth was incredible. For our study today, however, we will just look at one of His regular habits. Our Savior and Creator of this universe did something on a regular basis that really amazes me – He spent quality time alone with His Heavenly Father – God the Father.

> Our Savior and Creator of this universe did something on a regular basis that really amazes me – He spent quality time alone with His Heavenly Father – God the Father.

Look at some of the instances when Jesus drew away for quiet time with God the Father. Write down what takes place in each of these passages…

Chapter 1

Matthew 14:13-23

_____

_____

Luke 6:12-16

_____

_____

Isn't it awesome to think about how much our perfect Savior felt the desire to be alone with the Father? He often spent intimate time with God. Jesus would go up into the mountains or out into the gardens. He would look for a quiet time and a quiet place so that He could be alone with God the Father.

Why do you suppose Jesus thought it was important to draw away and spend some time alone with God the Father? How did it enhance His ministry?

_____

_____

> **Just as it benefited our Savior to spend time alone with God, so can it enrich our lives, too.**

Often, Jesus drew away with His Father just before a big event in His life. He prayed just before He chose His 12 disciples. He also stole away to the garden the night before His crucifixion. Jesus personally knew the benefit and the encouragement that came from time alone with His Father God.

Just as it benefited our Savior to spend time alone with God, so can it enrich our lives, too. I have found that when I spend time alone with my God, I have more peace, more courage, more joy, and a great deal more wisdom. When I face my family, my friends, my work, and the challenges of the day, I am better prepared to respond in a way that honors God if I've spent time alone that morning with Jesus.

My prayer is that you too will experience the incredible personal benefits of spending time alone with the Father. He wants to fill your life with joy, wisdom and great peace. He wants to prepare you for the day that's ahead as you spend time in His presence. Why not follow the Savior's example by drawing away from the crowds and spending time alone with your God.

What changes do you need to make to your schedule and lifestyle in order to allow you to be alone each day with God?

Look back over today's lesson and choose one Bible verse or part of a verse that you would like to focus on today.

> **My prayer is that you too will experience the incredible personal benefits of spending time alone with the Father.**

 Jot down your verse in the margin.

Day Two – Stepping Closer to Jesus by Looking into the Proverbs

....

 Warm-Up and Stretch

While yesterday's lesson was about our Model and how He spent time alone with God, today's lesson will encourage you to consider where, how, and when you might spend time alone with God.

As you begin today, take a few moments to pray. Ask God to speak to your heart. Invite Him to teach you new things that you've never seen or understood before.

Then, spend a minute in prayer using this verse as you pray, *"I thank You for speaking straight from Your heart; I learn the pattern of Your righteous ways." Psalm 119:7 (MSG)*

Exercise Your Spiritual Muscles

> "There is a time for everything, a season for every activity under heaven."
> Ecclesiastes 3:1 (NLT)

This first exercise may require you to actually get up and move. You may need to walk around a little as you consider some very practical questions.

After you read each question, take a minute to carefully consider your response.

1) <u>WHERE</u> can you go in your home to truly be alone with God?

- No distractions (TV, computer, laundry)
- You can be alone with as little noise as possible
- A place where you can relax and focus on God

This place is…

_____

> "Most of modern man's troubles come from the fact that he has too much time on his hands and not enough on his knees." *(14,000 Quips & Quotes)*

2) <u>WHEN</u> is the best time for you to have this time alone with God?

- No interruptions (kids, spouse, or even telephone if possible)
- A time when you can relax and focus on God without being too sleepy

This time is…

_____

> "We increase our ability, stability, and responsibility when we increase our sense of accountability to God." *(14,000 Quips & Quotes)*

3) <u>HOW MUCH TIME</u> will you start with – BE REASONABLE!

_____

- Start small and build up
- Give yourself the chance to get in the habit
- You can always add time

It will get easier as you practice.

The amount of time I'll start with is…

_____

Now, let's think about WHAT a person does during a quiet time alone with God. Most people do best when they have some sort of a guide or a plan – especially when just starting out. This isn't to make your time dry, but to give you some sort of a framework and a structure. Most quiet times involve prayer and time in God's Word.

> **Most quiet times involve prayer and time in God's Word.**

Begin today with a time of prayer. Get still and invite God to speak to you. Pray out loud if it helps!

Then, get your Bible and look up <u>Proverbs 2:1-12</u>. Read these verses over at least two times. Then, answer the following questions:

> **"If any of you lacks wisdom, let him ask of God, who gives to all liberally and without reproach, and it will be given to him."**
> **James 1:5 (NKJV)**

What is the main theme of this passage of Scripture?

_____

How does a person get wisdom?

_____

_____

Isn't it amazing that we can gain wisdom by just opening and reading God's Word? By seeking after His Word and searching out His wisdom, we are promised that we can find it. James 1:5 states, *"If any of you lacks wisdom, let him ask of God, who gives to all liberally and without reproach, and it will be given to him." (NKJV)*

God wants to generously give out His insights and His great wisdom. But, are we enjoying His generosity? Or, are we muddling around in our own human reasoning trying to get by?

What's the usual route you take to acquire great knowledge and understanding?

_____

_____

> "Tune your ears to wisdom, and concentrate on understanding. Cry out for insight and understanding. Search for them as you would for lost money or hidden treasure. Then you will understand what it means to fear the LORD, and you will gain knowledge of God." Proverbs 2:2-5 (NLV)

When talking with some of my closest friends, I've asked them how they make decisions and what they do in order to be wise. Some of my friends seek the counsel of a pastor or counselor. Others talk to all of their friends. One friend checks out the "self-help" books for her answers. However, my wisest friends always look to God and to His Word for wisdom. They may seek the help of advisors or friends, but the most mature Christians that I know ask God personally for His help. What about you?

Go back and read Proverbs 2:1-12 one more time. List 3-4 positive things that wisdom can do for you:

1) _____

2) _____

3) _____

4) _____

There are many benefits of wisdom that we find as we look through this passage. One that really stands out to me is the promise that God will be a "shield" and a "guard" for my life. He will guard my thoughts, my words, and my responses to my children, my life, and the paths that I take. Wisdom also provides understanding and gives us great joy.

Read Proverbs 2:2-5 in the margin. What encourages you most in these verses?

Look back over today's lesson and choose one Bible verse or part of a verse that you would like to focus on today.

 Jot down your verse in the margin.

$\mathcal{D}ay$ $\mathcal{T}hree$ – Stepping Closer to Jesus by Looking into the Psalms

....

 Warm-Up and Stretch

Once again, you will practice spending time alone with God today. This is your personal and private time with the Creator of the world! He loves to be with you, and He greatly enjoys your undivided attention!

1 John 4:15-16 tells us that *"All who confess that Jesus is the Son of God have God living in them, and they live in God. We know how much God loves us, and we have put our trust in His love." (Paraphrase of NKJV)*

> "I raise my eyes toward the mountains. Where will my help come from? My help comes from the Lord, the Maker of heaven and earth." Psalm 121:1-2 (HCSB)

 Exercise Your Spiritual Muscles

Begin your prayer time by literally looking up to heaven with your eyes open. Picture the Father lovingly looking down at you. Tell Him how you feel about Him right now. Pour out your heart to Him.

Psalm 62:8 reminds us to, *"Pour out your heart to Him, for God is our refuge." (NLT)* He is available twenty-four hours a day to listen to us talk. He never tires of hearing our voices or even of hearing the same old story over and over. He loves us and loves to spend time alone with us.

> **"Pour out your heart to Him, for God is our refuge." Psalm 62:8 (NLT)**

Get your Bible and open to <u>Psalm 121:1-8</u>.

Read over these verses a couple of times. Then, consider and answer the following questions…

Why do you think the Bible encourages us to "look up" or "raise our eyes"?

_____

_____

Take a moment right now and look up. Just turn your face up to heaven. Don't look around. Don't look out. Don't look inward. Don't look down. Instead, look up toward the Lord your God. There is something about physically looking up that absolutely transforms my perspective!

It's as if by looking up I am forced to turn my focus from myself and put it completely onto my Savior. Maybe this is why we are encouraged in the Bible to "look up"!

Now, read over the verses one more time. Then consider:

How has God helped you in the last few days?

_____

_____

What are two or three promises that encourage you in this Psalm?

_____

_____

Aren't you encouraged to know that God promises His help to us? I love knowing that God never sleeps; He is always watching over us and looking out for us. He is our Protector, our Shade, our Defender, and the One who guards us from all evil. We are indeed very blessed!

Go back over today's lesson and select a verse that encourages you.

Jot down your verse in the margin.

> Aren't you encouraged to know that God promises His help to us?

Day Four – Stepping Closer to Jesus in the Book of Luke

Warm-Up and Stretch

Congratulations! You've spent three days with the Lord this week! You are off to a great beginning. Today, we will look at a little more challenging passage. These verses will encourage you to take a good look into some of your relationships and some of your attitudes toward other people.

Begin with a moment of prayer. Pray this verse to the Lord, *"Father God, enable me to do what is right, to love mercy, and to walk humbly with You, my God."* Paraphrased from Micah 6:8 (NLT)

> "Father God, enable me to do what is right, to love mercy, and to walk humbly with You, my God." Paraphrased from Micah 6:8 (NLT)

Exercise Your Spiritual Muscles

As you prepare to read one of the great passages in the Bible about relating to others, ask God to speak to your heart. Take a few deep breaths. As you breathe, ask God to help you learn about better relationships as you look into His Word. Invite Him to help you identify any bad attitudes or anger that you need to get rid of today.

Now open your Bible to <u>Luke 6:27-36</u>. Read each verse twice very slowly. Then, respond to the questions:

What is this passage really talking about?

_____

_____

"Love your enemies! Do good to them! Lend to them! And don't be concerned that they might not repay. Then your reward from heaven will be very great, and you will truly be acting as children of the Most High, For He is kind to the unthankful and to those who are wicked. You must be compassionate, just as your Father is compassionate."
Luke 6:35-36 (NLT)

As you read Luke's words, you realize how relational he was. This passage gives us some great advice for dealing with people—even very difficult people. Most of us do have one or two people that act as sandpaper in our lives. Maybe it's a relative, a neighbor, or even a friend. Think for a minute about those people in your life that are difficult to deal with right now. Do you have anybody that challenges you and rubs you like sandpaper?

Is there anyone in your life that is difficult to love?

_____

If so, why are they so challenging to you?

_____

_____

Do you think others find you challenging to love? In what ways are you hard to love?

_____

_____

Look back over the passage one more time. What are two or three pieces of wisdom that you gain from this passage? Write your ideas in the blank space below:

The words of the Lord Jesus are tough in this passage-to love those that we consider to be our enemies, to return good for evil, to turn the other cheek. None of these are easy or even seemingly sensible, but they are straight from the heart of our Savior.

As I read these verses, I am personally challenged. It is especially hard for me as a mom to do good to those who hurt my children. You can mess with me, and I'll survive. But if you mess with my kids, then I can get downright mean! However, Jesus' words are pushing us to love and forgive even those people who hurt our family members. This is a challenge for most of us—an extreme challenge!

> When I consider the great compassion and patience of my heavenly Father towards me, who am I to demand my way?

However, when I consider the great compassion and patience of my heavenly Father towards me, who am I to demand my way? How about you? Have you experienced the love and the compassion of Almighty God? Then, think on His love and kindness next time you want to get even. Scripture promises a great reward in heaven if we act like "children of the Most High."

Go back and look over today's lesson. Find one key verse or part of a verse from today's lesson that you can take with you.

23

Jot down your verse in the margin.

Day Five – Stepping Closer to Jesus in the Book of 2 Corinthians

 Warm-Up and Stretch

> My prayer for you is that you will begin to be drawn to God's Word – that He will give you a love for the Bible and for spending time reading it, studying it, and getting to know it.

As you read and have time alone with God today, you will look at a very helpful passage in the Bible. God's Word is filled with such passages. These exercises are just a little sampling of all of the incredible "nuggets" and "jewels" contained in the Bible.

My prayer for you is that you will begin to be drawn to God's Word – that He will give you a love for the Bible and for spending time reading it, studying it, and getting to know it.

> "Give me an eagerness for Your laws rather than a love of money! Turn my eyes away from worthless things, and give me life through Your word."
> Psalm 119:35-36 (Paraphrased prayer from NLT)

Begin with prayer time. Ask God to show you something great in His Word today. Psalm 119 is filled with encouragement about loving and desiring God's Word. One passage that I encourage you to turn into a prayer is found in verses 36-37, *"Give me an eagerness for Your laws rather than a love of money! Turn my eyes away from worthless things, and give me life through Your word."* (Paraphrased prayer from NLT)

Exercise Your Spiritual Muscles

Open your Bible to <u>2 Corinthians 4:1-10.</u> Read this passage through at least two times.

In the Apostle Paul's day, pots and jars were made out of shells and then baked in a kiln. These containers were quite fragile and breakable. Paul compares these fragile vessels to our weak and fragile human bodies. We are men and women with feet of clay. Many days I don't just *feel* fragile; I feel like an absolute wimp!

Do you ever feel like a fragile clay jar or pot or a wimp? If so, how?

_____

_____

What events or situations typically make you feel the most fragile and weak? (Financial, relationships, work, etc.)

_____

_____

Describe a time in your life when you have experienced being pressed on every side. Perplexed. Hunted down. Knocked down.

Pressed on every side?

_____

_____

Perplexed?

_____

_____

Hunted Down?

_____

_____

Knocked Down?

_____

_____

Read the way that *The Message* paraphrases this passage. Underline each of the words or phrases that you can relate to personally today:

> "If you only look at us, you might well miss the brightness. We carry this precious Message around in the unadorned clay pots of our ordinary lives. That's to prevent anyone from confusing God's incomparable power with us. As it is, there's not much chance of that. You know for yourselves that we're not much to look at. We've been surrounded and battered by troubles, but we're not demoralized; we're not sure what to do, but we know that God knows what to do; we've been spiritually terrorized, but God hasn't left our side; we've been thrown down, but we haven't broken." 2 Corinthians 4:7-9 (MSG)

What is one verse or one portion of a verse that encourages you?

 Jot down your verse or verse portion in the margin.

Exercise tips of the week

~ Have a special time and place to meet with God each day. Designate this time & place.

~ Take it one day at a time. If you miss a day, don't despair. Just try again tomorrow!

Reviewing what we've learned

First...

Start each devotional time with prayer. Use a Bible verse to help you with this.

Second...

Open the Bible and read over one short Scripture passage. Read the verses at least two times.

Third...

Look for some practical information that you can use from these verses. Take notes as you read.

Fourth...

Choose one really good verse or part of a verse to "carry" around with you all day long.

Last...

Close your quiet time with prayer. Ask Him to help you to grow in your relationship with Him.

Why Do I Need to Study the Bible for Myself?

*D*uring college, I took an interesting class called "The Bible as Literature." The class examined the Bible as a great work of literature and art. We examined literary devices and word usage in Scripture and discussed the amazing beauty of God's Word. One passage we covered in detail was Psalm 19. In fact, the final exam included an essay all about Psalm 19.

Psalm 19 is a wonderful narrative that describes the greatness of God and the excellence of His Word – the Bible. The first six verses show the power of our Creator; the last eight verses detail the way God's Word can help and instruct us in His will for our lives. This Psalm was written by author and songwriter David.

This passage – Psalm 19:7-14 offers great reasons to open up and study God's Word. We discover how we will be blessed, helped, and encouraged by investing our time in Scripture.

Take a moment to read Psalm 19:7-14 as presented below:

> *"The law of the LORD is perfect, reviving the soul. The decrees of the LORD are trustworthy, making wise the simple. The commandments of the LORD are right, bringing joy to the heart. The commands of the LORD are clear, giving insight to life.*

Reverence for the LORD is pure, lasting forever. The laws of the LORD are true; each one is fair. They are more desirable than gold, even the finest gold. They are sweeter than honey, even honey dripping from the comb. They are a warning to those who hear them; there is great reward for those who obey them. How can I know all the sins lurking in my heart? Cleanse me from these hidden faults. Keep me from deliberate sins! Don't let them control me. Then I will be free of guilt and innocent of great sin. May the words of my mouth and the thoughts of my heart be pleasing to You, O LORD, my Rock and my Redeemer." (NLT)

Have you ever wondered or been asked, *"What's the big deal with the Bible anyway? What makes it so special? What makes it the greatest book ever written? Why are people always talking about Bible study?"*

> **The law of the Lord is perfect. The Bible is absolutely and completely perfect. It is total perfection.**

Let's consider some of the reasons God's Word matters and, look at why the Bible is an amazing, awesome book by reviewing the promises in Psalm 19. I pray that you will desire to open the Bible more after reading some of these promises. If you've just been away, I pray you'll dive back in again.

To begin with, Psalm 19:7 tells us, "<u>The law of the Lord is perfect.</u>" The word "perfect" comes from the Hebrew word "tâmîym," and it literally means to be entire, complete, without blemish, undefiled, and without a single spot. There is not one error or imperfection in God's holy Word. The Bible is absolutely and completely perfect. It is total perfection. *[2]*

Psalm 18:30 tells us, *"As for God, His way is perfect. All the LORD's promises prove true. He is a shield for all who look to Him for protection."* (NLT) God doesn't need touch ups, airbrushing, White Out, Photoshop or other types of correction devices. His Word is correct and right without any need for editing.

Because the Bible is perfect, we are promised that by reading it we will have our souls revived. The perfect and complete

Word of God revives, renews, and refreshes our hearts. *The Message* states Psalm 19:7 this way: *"The revelation of God is whole and pulls our lives together."*

His Word is somewhat like the musical tuner my daughter uses when she tunes her flute. She will activate her electronic tuner, and then adjust her flute to the perfect pitch of the tuner. Each time she plays, she has to get her instrument back into tune. Without the perfect pitch of her tuner, she cannot play the right notes. But, when she does get in tune, her notes are sweet.

> **"The Bible is a trustworthy book. The statutes of the Lord are trustworthy."**
> **Psalm 19:7 (NIV)**

Similarly when I open, read, and study the perfect Word of God, He is able to make my life right again. He is able to give me the perfect pitch and get me back into tune. I need the Bible to adjust my life so that the notes sound sweet as I "play" my instrument for Him.

We also need time in God's Word because <u>it is a trustworthy book</u>. According to Psalm 19:7, *"The statutes of the Lord are trustworthy."* (NIV) The word for trustworthy is the Hebrew word "'âman," and it means to build up or support; to foster as a parent or nurse; to be firm or faithful, to be permanent; to be true or certain. God's Word is absolutely trustworthy, a book that we can depend on without any hesitation or doubt. *[3]*

Psalm 62:7-8 in *The Message* encourage us with this, *"My help and glory are in God —granite-strength and safe-harbor-God—so trust Him absolutely, people; lay your lives on the line for Him. God is a safe place to be."*

Don't you love that picture? God is our safe harbor. Just as ships come into the harbor for safety from the ocean storms, we can go to the Lord and to His Word for safety in the storms of our lives.

My family grew up going to the lake. My father's job provided us access to boats and a lake house. From my early days in elementary school, I remember water skiing, inner-tubing, and riding on several different kinds of boats. Many summer days were spent out on the lake.

Every so often, a storm would blow in while we were out on the lake. When the clouds came over and the winds picked up, we would head toward the safety of the harbor and the boat docks. It was never fun or safe to be out on the lake in the middle of a large storm. When that rain starting pouring and that water started churning, we did not want to be out on the lake. We wanted to be in the safety of the docks.

> "My help and glory are in God —granite-strength and safe-harbor-God—so trust Him absolutely, people; lay your lives on the line for Him. God is a safe place to be."
> Psalm 62:7-8
> in *The Message*

God's Word can be that same sort of safe place for us. When we hear the thunder and feel the breezes of life start to pick up, we can go to the Bible for help and for encouragement. God's Word is like that boat dock – it is the safest place to anchor our lives in a storm.

Think about this for a minute…

- Do you have a "safe place" in your home during storms? If so, where?
- What about spiritually and emotionally – what is your safe harbor? A person? A place? The Bible?

There is another blessing that we are promised by trusting in God's Word. Look at the last part of Psalm 19:7, "*The statutes of the Lord are trustworthy, making wise the simple.*" (NLT) By opening and reading God's Word, we are given wisdom.

Proverbs 2:6-7 states it this way, "*For the LORD grants wisdom! From His mouth come knowledge and understanding. He grants a treasure of good sense to the godly. He is their shield, protecting those who walk with integrity.*" (NLT)

Some believe wisdom is just a form of intelligence. Others believe that wisdom is something that comes with time and life experiences. The Hebrew people believed that wisdom was learning from the Bible the difference between right and wrong and applying it to daily life.

When I was growing up, my pastor was a wonderful preacher named Adrian Rogers. He had many great quotes, but one thing he said about wisdom has stuck with me: he said that wisdom was simply *"seeing things from God's point of view." [4]*

When I spend daily time in God's Word, <u>He makes me wiser and fills me with greater understanding</u>. I begin to see my life more from His perspective. *The Message* simply states the promise this way, *"The signposts of God are clear and point out the right road." (Psalm 19:7)*

> When I spend daily time in God's Word, He makes me wiser and fills me with greater understanding.

So often, I will be praying through an issue, and God will lead me right to a verse that gives me clear direction. For example, I may be dealing with a difficult person in my life, and He will lead me to Proverbs 15:1, *"A gentle answer turns away wrath, but harsh words stir up anger."* (NLT)

Recently, I was in an awkward situation where someone was very upset with me; God cautioned me with this verse. I was reminded how a calm answer could soften this person's anger toward me. It was as if God, through the Holy Spirit, restrained me and helped me not to react in anger. I was wiser on that day because of God's Word.

God's Word is filled with practical words for living. Each day we can look to the Bible to supply us with insight for our daily life. It's not an old dusty book written thousands of years ago. Rather, it is a guidebook for our walk on this earth. In Psalm 25:5 we see this truth in David's prayer, *"Lead me by Your truth and teach me, for You are the God who saves me. All day long I put my hope in You."* (NLT) The truths of Scripture teach us and give us incredible wisdom.

A third reason to open God's Word and read it is that <u>the Bible is right</u>. Psalm 19:8 says, *"The precepts of the Lord are right."* (NIV) The Hebrew word for right is "yâshâr," and this word means to be straight and upright. Literally, God's

Word is level, straight, and not one bit off. There is nothing wrong with the Bible – not one thing. *[5]*

With time in His Word, we can walk a more level, straight, and upright path. But without time alone with Him in the Bible, we veer off, we lose our course. We are not able to stay on the straight and the level path. Isaiah 26:7 (HCSB) tells us that, *"The path of the righteous is level; You clear a straight path for the righteous."* In Psalm 27:11 (HCSB) we read, *"Because of my adversaries, show me Your way, Lord, and lead me on a level path."*

To illustrate this principle, I think of wall papering. Have you ever tried to hang wall paper in a room in your home or office? Have you tried to make it perfectly straight and level? I remember a time early in our marriage when my gracious husband offered to hang wallpaper in our little half-bath. The room had only a mirror, a toilet, and a pedestal sink. It was a very small room.

> The Bible is right. Psalm 19:8 says, "The precepts of the Lord are right." (NIV)

We chose the perfect pattern, measured the room, purchased all of the correct materials and wallpaper tools, and began the project. I tried to help, but the bathroom was only big enough for one person to be in it at a time. So, he ended up doing the bulk of the work.

When he had finished hanging all of the paper and the border, he came out shaking his head. He warned me that although he had measured all of the walls carefully, the paper was hanging a bit crooked. I went in the little bathroom to take a look and immediately noticed what he was talking about. Our new wallpaper looked great, but it was not perfectly level.

As we looked a little closer, we realized that the problem wasn't our tools or a lack of careful planning. Instead, our ceiling and our framing were not level making the wallpaper crooked as well. He had measured by the ceiling expecting it to be the perfect guide, but it was not quite right.

In our spiritual lives, we need a perfect guide, a straight "ceiling" by which to hang up the wallpaper of our lives. If our guide is not straight, level, and upright, our lives will not be either. When we measure our lives by the perfect and straight Word of God, we will be able to hang things more accurately.

Think about this for a minute...

- What do you use to help guide your life? A person? A book? The church? A pastor?
- How has God's Word been a level guide for you to pattern your life after?
- How could the Bible level you out personally?

We are promised in Psalm 19:8, *"The precepts of the Lord are right, giving joy to the heart."* (NIV) Looking to the right and level Word of God will give joy to our hearts. *The Message* states it this way, *"The life-maps of God are right, showing the way to joy."*

> **In our spiritual lives, we need a perfect guide, a straight "ceiling" by which to hang up the wallpaper of our lives.**

In other words, when I spend time in God's Word, He gives me great joy. In fact, the Bible will cheer us up to the very core of our beings. Spending time reading and, studying the Bible will fill the deepest recesses of my heart with a sense of hope and purpose. It will cause me to be merry, to find gladness, to discover encouragement.

> **When I spend time in God's Word, He gives me great joy.**

A fourth reason to get into the Bible is that it is clear. Psalm 19:8 says, *"The commands of the LORD are clear."* (NLT) The word for clear is the Hebrew word "bar," and it means to be choice, clean, clear, and pure. The Bible is a clear guide for our lives. According to Psalm 119:105, *"Thy Word is a lamp unto my feet and a light unto my path."* [6] (KJV)

Going to the Bible is much like turning on a light in a dark room. The light makes things clearer, helping us to see. When we open the Bible, we get direction, guidance, and wisdom to light our path for the day. But, when we neglect time in God's Word, it's as if we are walking through a dark room. We bump into furniture, stumble over things in the room, and bungle our way through trying to get to the light or to another room in the house. We need time in the clear Word of God just like we need continuous light in a dark house.

> Going to the Bible is much like turning on a light in a dark room. The light makes things clearer, helping us to see.

Further, we are promised something wonderful from this clarity of the Word of God. At the end of Psalm 19:8, we read, *"The commands of the LORD are clear, giving insight to life."* (NLT) When I spend time in the Bible, I gain personal insight for my life. I get insights about parenting, marriage, friendship, money, decisions, challenges, and so many other important and practical aspects of life.

So often, as I am reading the Bible and thinking about a certain verse, God will give me a deeper understanding into one of my children's lives. Or, He will give me an idea for how I can encourage a friend. He may use His Word to show me why someone is acting the way that he or she is acting. The more time I spend in His Word, the more perceptive I am.

Think about this for a minute…

- Have you ever had one of those moments when God used His Word to clearly speak to you and give you perception? If so, what happened?
- If not, wouldn't you like to hear more clearly from God and His Word?

> If you will spend time in His Word, you can also gain important life insights. God can make you more aware and perceptive about people and situations in your life as well.

If you will spend time in His Word, you can also gain important life insights. God can make you more aware and perceptive about people and situations in your life as well. He doesn't have any favorite students; He'll impart guidance and wisdom to any of His pupils who will listen closely. Even you!

According to Psalm 119:98-100, we can be smarter than our teachers and those who are much older than we are by spending time in the Word. This passage tells us, *"Your commands make me wiser than my enemies, for Your commands are my constant guides. Yes, I have more insight than my teachers, for I am always thinking of Your decrees. I am even wiser than my elders, for I have kept Your commandments."* (NLT)

Reading the Bible is positive also because <u>God's Word is pure</u>. Psalm 19:9 tells us, *"Reverence for the LORD is pure, lasting forever."* (NLT) The original word here is "tâhôr." This word means to be clean and pure in a physical, chemical, ceremonial, or moral sense. *[7]*

Another great verse that uses a similar word for pure is found in the New Testament in 1 Peter 2:2. It simply states, *"like newborn babies, long for the pure milk of the word, so that by it you may grow in respect to salvation."* (NASB) God's Word does not deceive. It is unadulterated and sincere. By opening the Bible, reading it, and studying it; we grow in our relationship to Jesus. We move from spiritual babies to become more mature believers.

God's Word is pure. Psalm 19:9 tells us, "Reverence for the LORD is pure, lasting forever." (NLT)

Psalm 19:9 also promises us that this pure and sincere <u>Word of God lasts forever</u>. Psalm 119:89 states, *"Forever, O Lord, Thy Word is settled in heaven."* (NKJV) The Bible endures forever. The Bible has been here in the past, the Bible is here for us now, and the Bible will be around for our children and grandchildren.

Be encouraged because the Bible is not some passing fad or the book of the month. It's not going to be on the best seller list for a little while and then pass along. God's Word will endure and last forever.

As I think about my own lifetime, I can personally relate to this. When I was born, I had six sets of grandparents and great-grandparents still living. I remember my great-grandfather reading the Bible and believing it to be the infallible, inerrant Word of God. I also recall all four of my grandparents reading and believing the Bible. My parents still read and believe in God's Word, as do my husband and I. And now, my teenage children read and

Be encouraged because the Bible is not some passing fad or the book of the month.

trust in God's Word. I pray that their children and many more generations to come in our family will trust in God and in His Word.

My point is this: I personally have witnessed five generations of my family enjoying the pure and sincere Word of God. It has lasted for my entire lifetime and that of the relatives I personally know. But, we are just one little snippet of time. God's Word was around long before I came on the scene and it will be around long after I am gone.

Think about this for a minute…

- What about for you: do you have any grandparents, great-grandparents, or other relatives who relied on the Bible? How do their lives encourage your life?
- What kind of Bible legacy do you want to leave for your children and grandchildren?

His word is true. In Psalm 19:9 we read, "*The laws of the LORD are true; each one is fair.*" (NLT) The Hebrew word for true is "'emeth," meaning to be assured, completely true, not one thing false. People have been trying to prove the Bible to be false for thousands of years. They've mocked it, taken it apart, rejected it, and tried to disprove it, but no one has succeeded. *[8]*

> His word is true. "God's reputation is twenty-four-carat gold, with a lifetime guarantee. The decisions of God are accurate down to the nth degree." Psalm 19:9. *(The Message)*

I like how *The Message* presents this verse: "*God's reputation is twenty-four-carat gold, with a lifetime guarantee. The decisions of God are accurate down to the nth degree.*"

Have you stood in the grocery line recently and read the headlines on the monthly magazines? So often, I find myself curiously thinking, "*Is that really true? Was Elvis really sighted living up in the mountains? Are those movie stars really about to get a divorce? Have aliens really landed up in Montana?*"

Maybe you've done the same thing – read the headlines and wondered what was true and what was just some fabrication used to sell magazines? We don't have to wonder about God's Word. We don't have to question it or second guess it. We can trust our God and His Word to be absolutely and completely true. There is not one false word in all of Scripture.

Even beyond that, we are promised that the <u>Bible is fair</u>. The last part of Psalm 19:9 simply states, *"The laws of the LORD are true; each one is fair."* (NLT)

This word for fair is an interesting word. In the King James Version of the Bible, the wording states that the Bible is, "righteous altogether." It's the Hebrew word *"tsâdaq,"* a forensic term that means you can test it, check it, measure it, and it will still come out clean and clear. *[9]*

> The Bible is fair. "The laws of the LORD are true; each one is fair." Psalm 19:9 (NLT)

It's like one of those crime scene investigation shows where they solve a case by compiling, testing, and scientifically going over all of the evidence. Investigators do not determine what happened until they have tested the evidence routinely and with the highest scrutiny. Saying the Bible is "fair" is like saying it has been scientifically tested and proven to be right. You can run it through every machine you have in your lab. Every single test will only further prove its validity and accuracy.

So how does this help you and me? When we open God's Word each day, we can absolutely trust that everything we read is completely right and true. There is nothing false, wrong, or incorrect. There will be no retractions written by the editor. The Bible is clean and clear.

There is no other book, magazine, newspaper, website, or news channel that can make such a claim. Many get close to perfection, many are fair, but none can be depended on for 100% fairness all the time and in every situation except the Word of God.

A ninth reason to get into God's Word is that <u>the Bible is something to be desired</u>. Psalm 19:10 states, *"They (Your laws) are more desirable than gold, even the finest gold."* (NLT) This word in the Hebrew is *"châmad,"* and it means to delight in, something that is greatly beloved, a delectable thing, delight, desire, goodly, lust. When we desire something, we really want it; we take delight in it, and are passionate about it. *[10]*

> **The Bible is something to be desired.**

What do you greatly desire? Chocolate? A vacation? A pay raise? Peace and quiet? A close friend? Romance? Love? Acceptance? To lose 20 pounds? All of us have things that we passionately desire and would love to have. Do we passionately desire and want to have more of God's Word?

We are told lastly that the Bible is not just desirable, but <u>it's also sweet</u>. Psalm 19:10 says about God's laws, *"They are sweeter than honey, even honey dripping from the comb."* (NLT) This Hebrew word for sweeter is *"mâthôq."* It simply means sweet, tasting good, and leaving a good taste in your mouth. *[11]*

> **Today, if we were making a food comparison, we might choose to say that the Bible is sweeter than chocolate or cheesecake or a hot fudge sundae.**

God's Word is compared to sweet tasting honey in the Bible. In the time that the Bible was written, honey was a wonderful delicacy and a sweet treat. Today, if we were making a food comparison, we might choose to say that the Bible is sweeter than chocolate or cheesecake or a hot fudge sundae. For me personally, I would have to say that the Bible is sweeter also than crème brulee.

But, do we really believe that? Do you and I really love the way the Bible "tastes" to us? Do we look as forward to reading the Bible as we do having a meal at our favorite restaurant? Do we enjoy time in God's Word as much as we enjoy the foods that we love?

I think the food comparison hits home for most of us, and it probably did as well in Bible days. Most of us are very passionate about food and about eating. I know that I am. God wants us to be passionate about the Bible and to enjoy "eating" from His table as well.

In fact, we find eating language relating to food throughout the Bible. Psalm 34:8 encourages us to, *"Taste and see that the LORD is good. Oh, the joys of those who trust in Him!"* (NLT) Psalm 119:103 states, *"How sweet are Your words to my taste; they are sweeter than honey."* (NLT) Jeremiah 15:16 puts it this way, *"Your words were found, and I ate them ,and Your words became to me a joy and the delight of my heart, for I am called by Your name, O Lord, God of hosts."* (NASB) 1 Peter 2:3 encourages us to, *"taste the kindness of the Lord."* (NASB)

Think about this for a minute…

- What sweet food might you use to complete the phrase: Your words are sweeter than _____?

- How is the Bible sweet and desirable to you?
- If it's not yet, would you like it to be?

The final reason to dig into God's Word is found in Psalm 19:11-14. We are warned by the Bible. As we read and study, we are enlightened, taught, reminded, and instructed. Verse 12 of Psalm 19 asks, *"Who can discern his lapses and errors? Clear me from hidden [and unconscious] faults."* (AMP)

> "Taste and see that the LORD is good. Oh, the joys of those who trust in him!" Psalm 34:8 (NLT)

Looking into the Bible daily is like looking in the mirror each morning. When we look in the mirror, we see better how to brush our hair, apply makeup, shave, and so many other grooming practices. Sometimes, we look in the mirror and like what we see. Other times, we find ourselves wishing for another mirror. Either way, the mirror daily reveals to us what is actually there.

> Looking into the Bible daily is like looking in the mirror each morning.

When I open the Bible, I learn what needs to be changed, fixed, improved, and even what looks good. I look into the Bible to see a clearer picture of my own heart and life. I am reminded, warned, and encouraged. Sometimes, I would rather look into the newspaper or a magazine, but I need the Bible. God's Word reveals the reality of my sin to me.

> "How can I know all the sins lurking in my heart? Cleanse me from these hidden faults. Then I will be free of guilt and innocent of great sin." Psalm 19:12-13 (NLT)

Psalm 19:12-13 puts it this way, *"How can I know all the sins lurking in my heart? Cleanse me from these hidden faults. Then I will be free of guilt and innocent of great sin."* (NLT) When I open the Bible, I see the truth about myself and my sin. I can't lie to God and to His Word just like I can't lie to my bathroom mirror. It reveals the truth of who I am. I can't change reality. The mirror shows my true self. Each morning my mirror reveals the good, the bad, and the parts that need some help.

Similarly, I can open the pages of God's Word to look inside and see my true self – the good, the bad, and the part that needs some help. Often, I will pray the words of this final verse in Psalm 19 as I open God's Word, *"May the words of my mouth and the thoughts of my heart be pleasing to You, O LORD, my Rock and my Redeemer."* (NLT)

There are so many benefits to spending time in God's Word. From daily reading and study in the perfect Word of God, we are refreshed and revived. The trustworthy Word of God makes us wise. The straightness and accuracy of the Bible can give us great joy.

> Maybe you are one of those who has struggled to spend time regularly reading and studying the Bible... What if you gave it another try?

The clarity of the Bible offers us insights for living this life. The pure Word of God is not a fad but rather a book that will last forever. We can count on the Bible to be completely fair and without one fault. God's Word is sweet to the taste and adds delight to our lives. And, finally, the Bible warns us, protects us, and keeps us on the right path.

As we draw this chapter to a close, we can acknowledge that personal Bible study is important. Spending time daily reading and thinking about the words of our Lord is great. But, for so many women, it's just not a normal practice – it's not something they regularly do.

Maybe you are one of those who has struggled to spend time regularly reading and studying the Bible. You want to and you mean to, but you just don't get around to it. What if you gave it another try? What if you took this next week and tried personal Bible study each day?

To sum up Chapter Two:

We open the Bible and read & study it for ourselves because:						
The Bible revives our souls.	The Bible makes wise the simple.	The Bible brings joy to the heart.	The Bible gives us insights for living.	The Bible lasts.	The Bible is sweet and desire-able.	The Bible both warns and pro-tects us.

Moving forward from here...

In Week Two, there are five days of personal Bible study. Each day you will have the chance to spend a few moments studying the Bible for yourself. The lessons are not long and they are not hard. They are just "appetizers" to tempt you to taste more freely of God's Word.

I pray that you will find the Bible to be desirable and sweet for yourself this week. May God give you such encouragement and hope as you open His Word!

STEP TWO: PERSONAL BIBLE STUDY

Try it for yourself!

Have you ever thought about what it might be like to move to another country? Maybe just another part of the United States? What would the people be like? What might be different for you?

One thing to consider is that you might not have a great deal of spiritual help and encouragement in another country or another part of the USA. My youth minister occasionally asked us to think about what it might be like to have only a Bible, pen, and some paper. What would we do to grow as a Christian? How would we learn more about God's Word?

He challenged us to know how to study God's Word on our own. Many retreats and camps were used as training times for studying God's Word. As a teenager, I learned how to be "fed" the meat of the Word if I only had a Bible, paper, and a pen.

You can learn to do the same thing. Sure, there are many wonderful Bible study guides available. There are incredible tools and resources available online and in local bookstores. However, there is no substitute for personal Bible study – just you, your Bible, and your God. Absolutely no substitute!

This week, we will focus on some very practical and easy ways that you can personally study God's Word on your own. These are just a small sampling of some great methods that are available. Try out each of these methods, and find one that is well suited for your time and personality.

This week's challenging question: If I had to be responsible for all of my spiritual "food," would I be well-fed or would I go spiritually "hungry"?

> If I had to be responsible for all of my spiritual "food," would I be well-fed or would I go spiritually "hungry"?

Day One –Personal Bible Study
– Try Tasting and Seeing

 Warm-Up and Stretch

Get still for a moment, and ask God to speak to you. Let Him know that you desire to learn to study His Word. Invite Him to give you a heart for His Word.

<u>Verses to pray</u> – *"Teach me Your decrees, O Lord; I will keep them to the end. Give me understanding and I will obey your instructions; I will put them into practice with all my heart. Make me walk along the path of Your commands, for that is where my happiness is found."* (Psalm 119:33-35, NLT)

 Exercise Your Spiritual Muscles

> **"There is no substitute for personal Bible study – just you, your Bible, and your God. Absolutely no substitute!"**
> Melanie Redd

Today, we will try a method that was taught for years by Pastor Adrian Rogers at Bellevue Baptist Church. This method has no real name, so I just call it the "Taste and See Method" from the verse *"Taste and see that the Lord is good. How blessed is the man who takes refuge in Him." Psalm 34:8* (NASB)

"<u>Taste and See Method</u>"... Basically, you will consider three questions. You can do this with any passage or chapter in the Bible. We will just take one passage and answer three questions about that passage.

<u>Passage to read</u> – <u>Joshua 1:1-10</u>

Question 1 – What did this passage mean back then – in Joshua's day?

_____

_____

I was one of those girls who played varsity basketball in high school. Before every game, our coach would give us a big pep talk encouraging us that we could defeat the other team. We went out onto the court for pre-game warm-ups ready to pounce on the other team and win the game. Our coach gave us our "marching orders" and told us to go for it.

Similarly, in Joshua 1:1-10, Joshua and the people are getting their pre-game pep talk. Their heavenly "Coach" is giving them their marching orders and telling them to go for it, to be strong and courageous.

> "Strength! Courage! Don't be timid; don't get discouraged. God, your God, is with you every step you take." Joshua 1:9 (MSG)

I especially love the way *The Message* states these marching orders, *"Strength! Courage! You are going to lead this people to inherit the land that I promised to give their ancestors. Give it everything you have, heart and soul. Make sure you carry out The Revelation that Moses commanded you, every bit of it. Don't get off track, either left or right, so as to make sure you get to where you're going. And don't for a minute let this Book of the Revelation be out of mind. Ponder and meditate on it day and night, making sure you practice everything written in it. Then you'll get where you're going; then you'll succeed. Haven't I commanded you? Strength! Courage! Don't be timid; don't get discouraged. God, your God, is with you every step you take." Joshua 1:7-9 (MSG)*

Question 2 – What does this passage mean now – to believers in our day?

_____

_____

As current day Christians, we also need to be given spiritual pep talks and marching orders from time to time. As we start each day, we can check in with our heavenly "Coach" and read from His play book, the Bible. He often encourages us and gives us hope for the challenges that lie ahead.

Have you gotten a "pep talk" lately? How about some "marching orders"?

Question 3 – What does this passage mean for you personally today? How can you apply it to your life?

_____

_____

On those days when I am feeling dismayed and uninspired, I often turn to this passage in Joshua. I can almost hear the Commander of heaven's armies shouting out, "Don't give up; don't lose heart; you can do this!" And, on those days, I am encouraged to just keep on keeping on. It's not the time to hang my head or to quit. It's time to get up, stretch out, warm up, and get out there and "play" in the game of life.

> Ask Him to instruct you and to encourage you throughout the day from the time you've just spent with Him.

Although it's been years since I've played for my high school coach, his encouragement and words of wisdom play on in my mind. I'm a better person and a better athlete because I was in his program.

Likewise, spending time with my heavenly "Coach" helps me to hear and recognize His voice throughout the day. I am a wiser and a better person when I've been in His presence. I play so much better when I follow His game plans and instructions!

Take a few minutes to pray before you get going today. Look back over the verses you just studied. Ask God to teach you from this passage you have just read. Invite Him to make these marching orders applicable in your life today. Ask Him to instruct you and to encourage you throughout the day from the time you've just spent with Him.

Look back over today's lesson and choose one Bible verse or part of a verse that you would like to focus on today.

Jot down your verse or verse portion in the margin.

Day Two – Bible Study by Seeking and Finding

....

 Warm-Up and Stretch

As you prepare to study today, ask God to give you fresh hope from His Word. Pray and invite Him to speak to your heart.

> "The most desirable time to read the Bible is as often as possible." *(14,000 Quips & Quotes)*

<u>Verses to pray</u> – *"You are my Refuge and my Shield; Your word is the source of my hope. Lord, sustain me as You promised, that I may live! Do not let my hope be crushed."* (Psalm 119:114 & 116) (Paraphrased from NLT)

 Exercise Your Spiritual Muscles

"<u>Seek and Find Method</u>"– For this method, you will be using the index or "concordance" in the back of your Bible. In the concordance, words are listed in alphabetical order much like in a dictionary, allowing you to look up a variety of concepts and ideas.

If your Bible does not contain a concordance, you might want to use the internet for this project. There are a couple of wonderful free sites that offer Bible tools for anyone to use. One such site is www.biblestudytools.com. Go to this site and look under the

"Key Word Search" section. Type in the word or words you want to study. You will be given several choices and ideas.

Look up the word "refuge" or "shelter." Your Bible concordance may include one or both of these words. Jot down 4-5 Bible references (locations) that are listed. Then, look up each of these references in your Bible, read the verse, and make any notes on what you find.

> **"God is our refuge and strength, always ready to help in times of trouble"**
> **Psalm 46:1 (NLT)**

This exercise should give you a great overview of how to study the use of a certain word in the Bible. If you're having trouble finding the particular verses, use the table of contents at the front of your Bible to assist you.

Word to Look Up and Study - "Refuge" or "Shelter"

Refuge: Deut 33:27 : The eternal God is your refuge, underneath are the everlasting arms.

Bible Reference

He will drive out your enemy before you, saying, 'Destroy him.'

Is 25:4
Ps 46:1
Ecc 1:4
Ps 61:4

Notes about this verse

God is eternal. He is our refuge, he protects us from any enemies.

Bible Reference

Ps 91:2

Notes about this verse

Bible Reference

50

Notes about this verse

_____

_____

Bible Reference

_____

Notes about this verse

_____

_____

So, what did you find? Anything new? Maybe a verse you'd never even seen before?

Isn't it amazing to look at a few verses on one topic or on one word? I love trying this practice as I study God's Word. It's like trying different desserts or finger foods at a holiday party or at a pot luck dinner. It's fun to just sample a little bit of this dish and a little bit of that dish. When you find one dish that is especially sweet or tasty, you can simply "sample" a whole lot of that one dish!

God's Word can likewise be enjoyed in little bites. As you taste a little verse here and a little verse there, you will often find a whole Psalm or a great passage that you want to "munch and munch."

Maybe you even discovered one such tasty or sweet Scripture "dish" today!

Close your time in God's Word by asking Him to show you which of these verses from this lesson that He wants you to focus on today.

Jot down your verse or verse portion in the margin.

Day Three – Personal Bible Study by Mixing and Matching

....

 Warm-Up and Stretch

> "Open my eyes to see the wonderful truths in your instructions." Psalm 119:18 (Paraphrased from NLT)

As you prepare to study today, ask God to teach you and instruct you in His Truth. Pray and invite Him to speak to your heart.

Verse to pray – *"Open my eyes to see the wonderful truths in Your instructions."* Psalm 119:18 (Paraphrased from NLT)

 Exercise Your Spiritual Muscles

"Mix and Match Method"– To utilize this method, you will need three or four translations of the Bible. A translation is most simply defined as a book's language. The Bible was originally written in Hebrew and Greek. Over the centuries, the Bible has been translated into many different languages so that everyone can read it in their own language.

> "But those who wait on the Lord shall renew their strength; they shall mount up with wings like eagles, they shall run and not be weary, they shall walk and not faint." Isaiah 40:31 (NKJV)

The King James Version is the translation that many people prefer. However, there are many other wonderful versions and translations available for you to read and study. It's very likely that you have more than one translation or version of the Bible in your home right now.

Look around to see if you can find at least three or four different Bible translations. If you cannot locate actual Bibles, go online and use the Internet as your resource. Just do a word search for "Bible translations." There are many sites that will freely give you the Bible in 10-15 different versions or translations.

For this exercise, try to use <u>at least three translations</u> of the Bible.

Your passage for study today is <u>Isaiah 40:26-31</u>.

Begin by looking up the above passage in your usual Bible. Read the passage in this Bible first. Then, you will move onto other translations.

He will never let us give up or give in

In your usual Bible, what did you discover? *NIV*

It is more clear than other, older versions of the Bible. I understand more of what it is saying.

In another translation, the ___*New Amer Standard*___ translation, what did you discover?

_____

_____

In another translation, the ___*King James*___ translation, *more powerful* what did you discover? *in*

They each state "the" same way that if you wait upon the Lord, He will renew your strength; you will mount up w/ wings like eagles; you shall run & not be weary; you shall walk & not faint

In another translation, the ___*NLT*___ translation, what did you discover? *best version of these verses*

Look to the Heavens, look at the stars. Looke what He created

_____

What did you gain from this type of study?

No matter how the Bible verse is worded, God is always the Creator of life, He is always our strength, and He will always carry us through the storms

On our honeymoon, my husband and I had the chance to go somewhere very exotic. My very generous father-in-law sent us on a trip to St. John's Island in the Caribbean. While we

53

were there, we tried the most wonderful concoction that I've ever tasted—fresh coconut fried shrimp. Yum!

Since that trip many years ago, we've tried these shrimp at other restaurants and in other cities. None seem quite as good as that Caribbean dish, but I still enjoy them and order them often.

Searching through different translations and paraphrases of the Bible is much like trying your favorite dish at another restaurant. It may taste a little different or be served with a different sauce, but it's still your favorite dish.

You might be most comfortable with your normal version or translation of the Bible, but sampling other versions can add interesting insight to a given passage, such as a word or a synonym that greatly increases your understanding. Try this Bible study method from time to time. It will greatly enhance and expand your insight into God's Word.

Now, go back and select one verse that you can take with you today.

 Jot down your verse or verse portion in the margin.

Day Four –Personal Bible Study using the Little Dab Will Do You Method

....

 Warm-Up and Stretch

Today, ask the Father to make you wise through His Word. Invite Him to make you wiser than you have ever been before.

Verses to pray – *"Oh, how I love Your instructions! I think about them all day long. Your commandments make me wiser than my enemies, for they are my constant guide. Yes, I have more insight than my teachers, for I am always thinking of Your laws. I am even wiser than my elders, for I have kept Your commandments."* Psalm 119:97-100 (Paraphrased from NLT)

 Exercise Your Spiritual Muscles

<u>"Little Dab Will Do You Method"</u> – This is a very simple and meaningful way to study God's Word. You will only be taking a very small bite today. This method can be used for any verse or verses.

> "The unfailing love of the LORD never ends! By His mercies we have been kept from complete destruction. Great is His faithfulness; His mercies begin afresh each day." Lamentations 3:22-23 (NLT)

The main idea of this type of study is to take in a very small amount of Scripture and think on that small amount. You won't try to read a long passage, but rather focus on a very few verses.

Begin by reading <u>Lamentations 3:22-23</u> in the box.

Read these verses twice.

What is your first thought?

His love is unfailing and endless.

Read the verses again. What words stand out to you in this passage?

unfailing love, His mercy keeps us from complete destruction. His mercy begins new each day.

55

He loves me endlessly.

Read the passage again. What do you feel like God is saying to you personally today?

He will have mercy on me daily, He will never look down on me for my sins from the day before.

This is one of those little passages that encourages my heart! Knowing that God's mercies are fresh every single morning is one of those promises that makes me sleep better at night. Knowing that my God is faithful every single day and that His mercies never fail—these things absolutely blow me away.

Close your time in God's Word with a brief time of prayer. Share with God your needs, concerns, and challenges that you face today. Ask Him to speak "peace" over your life and these issues today.

Invite God to give you a verse to carry with you all day long.

 Jot down your verse or verse portion in the margin.

Day Five –Personal Bible Study by Making Lists

....

 Warm-Up and Stretch

Pray as you begin and ask God to show you more about how to get along with other people. Let Him know that you want to be wiser in dealing with family, friends, neighbors, and co-workers.

Verses to pray – *"Help me to let loyalty and kindness <u>never leave</u> me! Enable me to tie them around my neck as a reminder. Write them deep on my heart. <u>Free me to find favor with both God and people, and enable me to earn a good reputation."</u>* Proverbs 3:3-4 (Paraphrased from NLT)

 Exercise Your Spiritual Muscles

"<u>List and Learn Method</u>" – To use this method, you only need to be able to make a good list. There are some wonderful passages in God's Word that are full of lengthy lists. Sometimes, it helps us to break down the information by just making a list as we read and study. So, today, that is what you will be doing.

Begin by turning in your Bible to <u>Romans 12:9-21</u>. Read through these verses two times.

Then, answer the following questions:

Who is writing the words in this letter?

The Apostle Paul

To whom are these words written?

to Brothers & Sisters in christ, and also possibly to Brothers&Sisters who have yet to be saved, to give their bodies as holy sacrifices, Pleasing to God.

Isn't it amazing that the same book that addresses some really heavy and complicated theological issues in the early chapters then turns to some practical instruction in the last few chapters! As the Apostle Paul writes this letter to the believers in Rome, he very honestly talks to the people about how they relate to and deal with each other.

Read back over the list of statements that Paul makes in this little passage of Scripture.

Make a list of the challenges that are being given in this passage: (Try to list at least 5-6 items.)

Honor one another above self

* ~~Give graciously~~ Patience in affliction

Faithfulness in prayer

Bless those who persecute me

* Do not take revenge

* Feed the enemy if hungry *kill w/ kindnes

* Return evil with good

What a list! There are some items on this list that really challenge my heart and my lifestyle. Things like: loving people with authenticity, giving preference to other people, persevering in tough times, blessing those who are unkind, serving in humility, returning good for evil, being at peace with everyone, and not taking revenge on others. These are some tough commands to put into practice.

Look back at the list that you made. Put a star beside the 3 hardest commands for you to follow.

Why do you suppose these "starred" commands on the previous page are such a personal challenge for you?

It is so hard to go through hard times with faith in him, faith that He will pull me through no matter how hard it is at the time. My enemies are already hard to please before they become enemies. Then, once I dislike them, it is extremely tough to love them, despite what God says to do

What is one thing that you have gained from making this list today?

I know exactly what to pray for to help myself w/ hard & challenging commands that I must follow for God's glory.

Go back over the list and ask God to show you one of these commands that He'd like you to focus on today. Pray and ask God to enable you to gain some real victory in this area and to help you to make some progress.

Jot down your challenge in the margin.

How to understand a Bible passage:

> *"Read it through. Think it clear. Write it down. Pray it in. Live it out. Pass it on."*
> *-Dr. Adrian Rogers*

Exercise tips of the week

~ The Internet is filled with some wonderful and free Bible study resources. You can do a word search to find these materials.

~ Bible study does not have to take hours. You can gain great wisdom from being in God's Word for only a few moments each day.

~ There are a myriad of Bible study methods. You can use any of these methods to help you to get more out of God's Word.

~ Often the more you study the Bible, the more you will want to study the Bible. Give it a try.

Reviewing what we've learned

First ...	*Second ...*
Find a Bible translation that you can read and understand easily.	Choose a passage or chapter to read and study in the Bible.

Third ...	*Last...*
Select a method with which to study the passage. Use one from this study or come up with one of your own.	Pray and ask God to teach you as you study. Then dig in and discover some "gems" in the Word.

CHAPTER 3

What's the Big Deal with Prayer?

I was standing at the meat counter waiting on my turkey when she walked up. I smiled at her and asked her how she was doing. This woman – a total stranger – began to share her hurts with me right there in the grocery store. I stood and listened and nodded for a few minutes wondering why she was sharing her heart with me and in such a public place.

After offering her a brief word of encouragement, we parted ways and I headed to the checkout counter. As I pushed my cart across that store, a thought came to me: people are hurting everywhere. Whether divorce, illness, loneliness, wayward children, job loss, or anything else that may enter our lives; there is so much pain and hurt in all of our worlds.

What do we do with the hurt? What do we do when tragedy strikes or we experience broken hearts and lives? And, how can we help others when they are hurting? What can we say to our friends, relatives, children, spouses, and co-workers when they share their pain with us?

Sometimes, we need to seek out help. It may come in the form of a godly friend who will listen, love on us, and pray with us. Help may also come in the form of a wise Christian counselor who will give us Biblical guidance.

We also may find help we need from a medical doctor. It may be that we just need a good night of sleep or a vacation.

> The Message encourages us to "pray all the time."

Above all earthly help, however, I have found encouragement from one little verse in the Bible. 1 Thessalonians 5:17 simply states, *"Pray without ceasing." The Message* encourages us to *"Pray all the time."*

How do we practically do this? Can you really pray all the time? Can anyone? Many of us pray over meals, pray in church, pray before bed, and maybe talk to God a few other times during the week. But, how does a person pray without stopping?

We can pray all of the time by living in a spirit of prayer. This is a spiritual sounding phrase that literally means to keep the channels open with heaven all the time. Don't ever hang up the phone or disconnect from your heavenly Father.

Think of it in terms of modern communication. For years the telephone has been the primary form of communication for most people. However, in recent days, people are using text messages and emails to keep in touch with each other. My teenagers love to "text" their friends. It's like they never hang up; they just keep a day-long conversation going on in choppy, little sentences.

My husband loves to communicate via Twitter – a fast emailing service on his phone. All day and night people send him "tweets" telling him where they are and what they are doing. He responds by "tweeting" back and sharing the same. He doesn't have to dial up or disconnect; he just has to turn on his cell phone.

We can pray without ceasing by "tweeting" and "text messaging" with our heavenly Father. We can stay in constant communication with Him, checking in all day and all night. We never have to hang up or disconnect with God. And, He never hangs up or disconnects from us. His line is always open.

Let's take this a little further and look at what it might look like to spend an entire day in prayer – to pray without stopping for an entire day. You may be surprised to find how normal and natural prayer can become in your life.

<u>Start in the morning by waking up in prayer</u>. Look up to heaven and tell Him, "Good Morning!" Acknowledge Him as you begin your day. Make your morning prayer time a part of your daily routine. Just as you shower, dress, eat breakfast in the morning, and try also to spend a few moments talking to your Father.

> **Start in the morning by waking up in prayer.**

Check out the following poem written by *Bishop Ralph Cushman:*

"<u>God in the morning</u>"

"I met God in the morning
when the day was at its best;
And His Presence came like sunrise,
Like a glory in my breast.
All day long the Presence lingered,
All day long He stayed with me,
And we sailed in perfect calmness
O'er a very troubled sea.
Other ships were blown and battered,
Other ships were sore distressed,
But the winds that seemed to drive them,
Brought to me a peace and rest.
Then I thought of other mornings,
With a keen remorse of mind,
When I too had loosed the moorings,
With the Presence left behind.
So, I think I know the secret,
Learned from many a troubled way:
You must seek Him in the morning
If you want Him through the day!" *[12]*

A second way we can make prayer a natural part of our day is to <u>check in throughout the day with Him</u>. As you are stuck in traffic, while shopping, exercising, or as you are taking a break at work, you can pray for a moment or two. You and I can take little moments to look to the Lord. Just like those short text messages or emails, we can send a quick message to God or ask Him to send us one.

Check in throughout the day with Him.

What might this look and sound like in normal, everyday life? Prayer can take so many forms, and I'd like to mention just a few for you to consider and try. One form of prayer is petition – asking God for something. We can simply make requests and ask for His help. This is the easiest and probably the most common for most people.

We can ask for tangible things – a job, a raise, a home, a car, help with college tuition, or money to pay off all of our bills. We can pray about the intangible things – friendship, joy, peace, wisdom, discernment, and such. Some people ask for smaller things – a parking place, a date, or a good day. I even have one sweet friend that prays over her very curly hair. She asks God to give her "good hair days!"

Philippians 4:6 says, "Don't worry about anything; instead, and pray about everything. Tell God what you need, and thank Him for all He has done." (NLT)

I love the verse that tells us we can talk to God about everything. Philippians 4:6 says, *"Don't worry about anything; instead, pray about everything. Tell God what you need, and thank Him for all He has done."* (NLT)

Another form of prayer is thanks. We can take the time daily to just look up to heaven and say, "Thank you!" Expressing our gratitude and appreciation to our generous God is a wonderful way to pray.

In Luke 17, we find the story of the Lord Jesus healing ten men from the terrible disease of leprosy. They cried out for His help and His mercy, and He healed them as they walked to the temple. Ten were healed, but only one of the lepers came back to say, "Thank you." Jesus simply asked him, *"Where are the other nine?"* Luke 17:17 (NIV)

We can be like that one man who came back and thanked Jesus for what He had done. Thanksgiving is like writing a thank you note to God or sending Him an email of thanks. Throughout the day, we can take a moment to utter a quick "thanks" for safety, for sunshine, for good health, for life, for freedoms, for friendship, for that new grandbaby, and for so many millions of other things.

Think about this for a minute…

- What are 10 things you could stop and thank God for right now? Why don't you do it?
- How has He been good to you and to your family?

We can also pray without ceasing by offering praise to God. Praise is like thanks but includes expressing approval and admiration to God for who He is. It's telling Him how great and amazing we think He is.

How do we do this? We can look at the beauty of a sunset and tell God how awesome He and His creation are. As we see a newborn child, we can marvel at His handiwork and creativity. When we receive a gift or an act of kindness, we can praise God for being our Provider.

> **When we receive a gift or an act of kindness, we can praise God for being our Provider.**

One very easy way to offer praise to God is to use the alphabet when you pray. For the letter "A," you can praise God for being amazing, almighty, and awesome. For the letter "B," you can praise God for being near, for His bigness, and for His brilliance. Continue through the rest of the alphabet praising God in this way.

Another way to keep in touch all day long with our God is to repent. As needed, we confess to Him anything that we need to make right. When He brings something to mind, we can agree with Him and immediately get it right. He may nudge us to turn off the TV or to get off the Internet. He may urge us to apologize to someone. He may remind us to make a phone call that we need to make.

Confession may involve tears and grief; but I have found that by checking in often during the day with Him, I avoid all kinds of problems. I keep short accounts and stay current with

65

God. When I do this, I live with more freedom and joy. And, it seems that the more I check in with Him, the less I have to repent of!!!

It's sort of like paying the bills. In our home, I'm the one who receives, keeps up with, and pays off the monthly bills. With the help of some wonderful computer software, I enter the credits and the deposits at least twice per month. Staying consistent makes the whole process so much easier. However, sometimes life gets busy and I miss a few weeks. When I do this, it takes me forever to pay the bills and reconcile the checking account.

> My prayer for you is that you will make confession and repentance part of your daily schedule... If you will check in often with your heavenly Father, you too will keep shorter accounts and find greater joy and freedom in your life.

My prayer for you is that you will make confession and repentance part of your daily schedule. Check in with God often and ask Him if there's anything He'd like for you to reconcile or fix. If you will check in often with your heavenly Father, you too will keep shorter accounts and find greater joy and freedom in your life.

Making appeals to God is another type of prayer. Just as a lawyer or a defendant might make an appeal in a courtroom, we too can earnestly request help from our heavenly Judge. Appealing is revisiting a concern or a topic for the 3rd or 4th or 100th time. It's laying out our requests with great passion and emotion.

My kids have the practice of appealing down to a science. When they really, really want to do something, they make sure we know. They will ask us, plead with us, reason with us, beg us, and even bug us if they think it will help. Both of my children know how to earnestly ask for what they need and want.

The Lord Jesus addressed this topic of appealing during His Sermon on the Mount. In Matthew 7:7-11, He instructs the people, *"Keep on asking, and you will be given what you ask for. Keep on looking, and you will find. Keep on knocking, and the door will be opened. For everyone who asks, receives. Everyone who seeks finds. And the door is opened to everyone who knocks. You parents – if your children ask for a loaf of bread, do you give them a stone instead? Or if they ask for a fish, do you give them a snake? Of course not! If you sinful people know how to give good gifts to your children, how much more will your heavenly Father give good gifts to those who ask Him?"* (NLT)

How long do we make appeals to God about something? Is there a time to stop asking? You should ask until one of two things happens: 1) God grants your request and gives you what you are asking for, or 2) God changes your desire and gives you the peace to let it go. Pray until you have an answer or until you are okay with a closed door.

> "God will either give you what you want or He will change your 'wanter!'"
> **Dr. Adrian Rogers**

My pastor growing up, Dr. Adrian Rogers used to have some great instruction about praying in earnest. He put it this way, *"God will either give you what you want or He will change your 'wanter!'"* This is not an easy concept to grasp, whether you've been walking with Jesus for a short while or a long time. But, my encouragement to you is to keep appealing to God about your situation until He answers your prayer or gives you the grace to stop asking. You will either become "okay" with your issue or He will work it out for you somehow. *[13]*

Jesus taught the people so many amazing things while He was here on earth. In one such message, He addressed prayer. Listen to His words in Luke 11:9-10, *"And so I tell you, keep on asking, and you will be given what you ask for. Keep on looking, and you will find. Keep on knocking, and the door will be opened. For everyone who asks, receives. Everyone who seeks, finds. And the door is opened to everyone who knocks."* (NLT) Keep knocking, seeking, and asking until you get some sort of answer – positive or negative.

There's another form of prayer that we can utilize when we pray without ceasing. It's prayer by crying out to God. To cry out is to express the deepest hurts, needs, desires, passions, and wishes of your heart to your loving heavenly Father. You may cry, scream, whisper, groan, or simply look up and say "help!"

One of my dear friends cries out by walking around her house talking out loud to God. She goes from room to room pacing and talking things over with God. Sometimes she is loud, sometimes she is quiet, sometimes she is happy, and other times she is in anguish. No matter her mood, her regular practice is to cry out to God.

> **"Therefore the LORD longs to be gracious to you, and therefore He waits on high to have compassion on you. For the LORD is a God of justice; How blessed are all those who long for Him." Isaiah 30:18 (NASB)**

Our God is so good and merciful and patient and gracious! He loves us with unconditional and unfailing love. Isaiah 30:18 encourages us with, *"Therefore the LORD longs to be gracious to you, and therefore He waits on high to have compassion on you. For the LORD is a God of justice; How blessed are all those who long for Him."* (NASB)

We can also take great hope from the words of Hebrews 4:14-16, *"Now that we know what we have - Jesus, this great High Priest with ready access to God - let's not let it slip through our fingers. We don't have a priest who is out of touch with our reality. He's been through weakness and testing, experienced it all - all but the sin. So let's walk right up to Him and get what He is so ready to give. Take the mercy, accept the help."* (The Message)

Daisy is this great big fluff ball that lives with us. She is some sort of a Collie mixed with some sort of a Husky. Her coloring is Collie, but her bark and the way she "talks" are totally Husky. When in the back yard, she stays on a tie-out made just for big dogs like her. Often, she paces around the trees in our yard and gets completely and utterly twisted and stuck. Sometimes we will find her just inches from the trunk of some tree she has gotten wrapped around.

In her panic and frustration, she will begin to groan and cry out. She doesn't bark, but she sort of "cries" for us to come and free her. When we hear her cries, we know what has happened. And, if we step out onto the back porch, she'll begin to "talk" to us about her stuck condition. She'll cry out and groan until we walk over and actually free her. Even on the busiest of days, I am alert to Daisy's cries. Our God is the same way. Even when He is overseeing disasters and catastrophes and needs all over the planet, He still is aware of your cries and mine.

Another way to pray all through the day is just by <u>thinking about our great God</u>. We can silently direct our thoughts and our prayers to Him constantly without ever speaking out loud. To turn our ears and eyes toward heaven is to focus on Him.

Just before a big meeting, speech, class, or tough situation, we can silently speak a quick prayer to the Lord. When we see ambulances go by, we can pray quietly for those in need. In the middle of a hard conversation, we can silently ask God for help. If we are about to spend time with a hurting friend, we can silently pray for extra mercy and wisdom. When we are ready to "slay" one of our children, we can silently pray for patience and restraint.

> We can silently direct our thoughts and our prayers to Him constantly without ever speaking out loud.

<u>Think about this for a minute</u>...

- Do you find yourself thinking about God during the day?
- How often do you communicate silently with your heavenly Father during the day or night?
- How might your attitude change if you did this more regularly?

There's another great way that we can communicate with God throughout the day. It's to <u>sing to Him</u>. For some of us this is more of a joyful noise, but for others it is a beautiful melody. Whether or not you can sing, you can sing to the Lord. You can hum, whistle, enjoy the music, or sing at the top of your lungs.

Prayer and worship with singing are mentioned throughout the Bible. In Psalm 13:6, we read, *"I will sing to the LORD because He has been so good to me."* In Psalm 40:3, we hear, *"He has given me a new song to sing, a hymn of praise to our God. Many will see what He has done and be astounded. They will put*

69

their trust in the LORD." (NLT) In Psalm 95:1, we are told to, *"Come; let us sing to the LORD! Let us give a joyous shout to the rock of our salvation!"* (NLT) And, in Psalm 104:33, we read, *"I will sing to the LORD as long as I live. I will praise my God to my last breath!"* (NLT)

> **"I will sing to the LORD as long as I live. I will praise my God to my last breath!" Psalm 104:33 (NLT)**

Often, we can just think about the words of a great song and enjoy the music with God. As you are driving in the car, turn to some praise or inspirational music. The words alone will encourage you to think about the Lord. As you are cleaning house or working out, turn on some praise music and sing along.

If you are having a hard day, tune in your computer to a great Christian music station or website. The lyrics can point you back to your Savior. The music can lift you out of the depths.

> **Many days I will pray and ask God to enable me to really listen. I ask Him to not let me miss Him and His work in my life.**

As you continue to pray without stopping, try to listen for God to speak to you. <u>Listening is another form of prayer.</u> As we pay attention to what is going on around us, tune in, and make every effort to hear from God; I believe that we will. He may speak to us through the words of a friend, through a sermon, through music, through a sunset, or through His Word.

Just as we tune in to a certain radio station, we can tune our hearts and our spirits toward heaven. We can make ourselves attentive to the fact that God is still at work all around us. According to Matthew 13:15-16, we need to soften our hearts and be open to the work of God in our lives, *"For the hearts of these people are hardened, and their ears cannot hear, and they have closed their eyes – so their eyes cannot see, and their ears cannot hear, and their hearts cannot understand, and they cannot turn to me and let me heal them. Blessed are your eyes, because they see; and your ears, because they hear."* (NLT)

Many days I will pray and ask God to enable me to really listen. I ask Him to not let me miss Him and His work in my life. Recently, I was praying over a very big issue for our family.

My heart was especially heavy on one particular week. Every single time I turned on Christian radio that week, I heard the same song by the group Hillsong. The words simply say, *"Savior, He can move the mountains, my God is mighty to save, He is mighty to save."*

Each time I heard those words, it was as if God was whispering the words for me personally to hear. He was telling me, *"I am mighty to save. I am your Savior. I can move this mountain!"* I know that I heard that song at least seven times that week. It was playing every single time I turned on my computer or my car. I believe that God was speaking directly to me.

<u>Think about this for a minute</u>...

- Have you ever felt like your heavenly Father was "speaking" to you?
- How has He "spoken" to you personally?
- How does it encourage you to know that the God of this universe wants to communicate daily with you?

There's one final way we can practice ongoing prayer. It's to <u>breathe a prayer</u> to God. Just like we breathe in air and breathe out Carbon Dioxide, so also we can breathe in a little bit of heaven and breathe out a little bit of earth.

This form of prayer is somewhat like crying out, but it is quieter. Rather than groan or yell or cry, we just simply get still and quiet in the presence of the Lord. We get still, take deep breaths, think about the Lord, and just breathe in the nearness of our God.

It's much like breathing in the aroma of a great food as you walk into your favorite restaurant, or breathing in the fresh air at the beach or the lake. The deeper you breathe, the more you enjoy the aroma. Similarly, when we get still and "breathe in" the Lord Jesus, we enjoy Him. As we focus our attention on Him, we experience a sweeter and more personal relationship with Him.

Have you ever had the chance to be in the hospital with a dear, old saint as they were breathing their last breaths? Often, they can't say much or do much except to lie back on the bed and wait to breathe their last breath. But, as they get close to stepping over into eternity, many of them will begin to smile. It's as if they are breathing in more and more of heaven and less and less of this old earth.

The Psalmist in Psalm 116:1-2 encourages us with this promise, *"I love the LORD because He hears and answers my prayers. Because He bends down and listens, I will pray as long as I have breath!"* (NLT) Don't you love the picture of God leaning down and listening to our very last breath of prayer?

> **You can close out the day talking with Him.**

Praying all day can be practiced in so many different ways and forms. We can ask, offer thanks, praise, repent, make an appeal, cry out, sing to God, think about Him, listen for Him, and just breathe Him in all day long.

Finally, after spending all day praying and communicating with your heavenly Father, you can <u>close out the day talking with Him</u>. Take a few moments to reflect on the day with Him. Talk over any details that you need to with Him. Some people like to use a journal to write out these prayers. Then, tell Him how much you love Him and say, *"Good night."*

That's what it means to pray without ceasing – get a strong connection going in the morning and keep it going all day long. Life is hard! Some days and weeks and months, life is really tough! The best advice I have -- Pray without stopping!

To sum up Chapter 3:

We can pray without ceasing by...		
Starting our day with Him each morning.	Spend your day with Him... Asking, Thanking, Praising, Confessing, Appealing, Crying Out, Singing, Listening, Thinking of Him, and Breathing Him in and out all day long.	End your day by talking to Him & telling Him, "Goodnight."

Moving forward from here...

This week – ask God to blast open your prayer life and to bring a whole new meaning to praying without ceasing!! Try out the exercises for Step Three. Allow God to increase and enlarge your personal prayer life as you make more time for Him.

STEP THREE: PRAYING

Try it for yourself!

Go to any bookstore or website, and you'll find thousands of books on prayer. Weekly, ministers and pastors all over the world passionately preach about prayer. Churches have prayer rooms, prayer lists, prayer groups, and so many programs that encourage prayer.

And yet, for most people, prayer is just not a big part of our daily lives. Yes, we pray a little as we start the day, as we drive to work or school, and as challenges arise. But, are we men and women of prayer? Are we growing in our prayer lives? Is prayer an integral part of our lives?

This week's lessons will give you some very practical ways to implement prayer into your life. Each day you will study one component of prayer. As you practice each type of praying, you will hopefully become more comfortable and more adept in your prayer life.

This week's challenging questions – What do you think of when you hear the words "prayer warrior?" Would you say that you are a person of prayer? Even a prayer warrior?

Day One – Try Praying with Praise

....

 Warm-Up and Stretch

> "Prayer is a little bit like eating salted peanuts; the more you do it, the more you want to do it." *(14,000 Quips & Quotes)*

Praise in its simplest terms is acknowledging God for being God. It's that moment when we take our eyes off ourselves and "look up" into the face of our amazing God. Psalm 121:1-2 simply says, *"I look up to the mountains – does my help come from there? My help comes from the LORD, who made heaven and earth."* (NLT)

Praise is also honoring and adoring God for who He is.

God loves to be praised. Scripture tells us that He inhabits the praise of His people (Psalm 22:3, KJV). It's as if He draws up close and has a seat when we are expressing our love and affections for Him. Just as I love to hear praise and gratitude from my own children, our heavenly Father also loves to hear our expressions of gratefulness.

Grab your Bible and a pen, and let's get started.

 Exercise Your Spiritual Muscles

Look up these verses about praise below. Then, write each passage into a prayer of praise in your own words. Voice this prayer aloud to God after you write it down. Take time to express your love and gratitude to your heavenly Father.

Psalm 18:1-3

_____

_____

Isaiah 40:26-31 (New Living Translation)

26 Look up into the heavens.
Who created all the stars?
He brings them out like an army, one after another,
calling each by its name.
Because of his great power and incomparable strength,
not a single one is missing.

27 O Jacob, how can you say the LORD does not see your troubles?
O Israel, how can you say God ignores your rights?

28 Have you never heard?
Have you never understood?
The LORD is the everlasting God,
the Creator of all the earth.
He never grows weak or weary.
No one can measure the depths of his understanding.

29 He gives power to the weak
and strength to the powerless.

30 Even youths will become weak and tired,
and young men will fall in exhaustion.

31 But those who trust in the LORD will find new strength.
They will soar high on wings like eagles.
They will run and not grow weary.
They will walk and not faint.

Now, look up these verses and write them as a prayer of praise.
Try to put the verses into your own words.

Psalm 145:8-9

_____

_____

For Psalm 145:8-9, I might have written my prayer out like
this, "Thank you, God, for being all mercy and grace. Thanks
for not being quick to get angry. I really appreciate Your love
and Your patience. I praise You also for Your goodness to every
single person." I try to take the words of the Scripture and
make them mine. Then, I pray them back to the Lord.

I think He really enjoys hearing His words spoken
by His children. I know that I love to hear my two
children repeat something good or wise that I have
taught them. It makes me feel like I just might be
doing a decent job of parenting. God also loves to
hear us using, repeating, and praying His words.
It must warm His heart to hear us speak the very
words that He has spoken to and for us!

> "The LORD is
> righteous in all His
> ways and kind in
> all His deeds. The
> LORD is near to all
> who call upon Him,
> To all who call upon
> Him in truth." Psalm
> 145:17-19 (NASB)

Try a few more of these verses:

Psalm 145:13-14

_____

_____

Psalm 148:1-6

_____

_____

Psalm 150:1-6

_____

_____

A few years ago, a younger girlfriend of mine called and asked if she could use something I'd taught her to teach some other ladies. She liked an illustration that I had used, and she wanted to pass it along to a Bible study she was leading. Of course I gave her permission to use the illustration. But, more than that, I was encouraged that she had heard the truth and remembered the applications from God's Word.

I was so happy that she wanted to share my ideas with others. Similarly, I believe our heavenly Father is happy when we remember His truths, apply them to our lives, and desire to share them with others.

Why don't you read back over the lesson today, and ask God to give you one truth that you can take, apply, and share with someone else today? Invite Him to speak to your heart with a specific verse or principle.

 Jot down your verse or principle in the margin.

Conclude your Bible study and praise time by telling God how much you love and appreciate Him. Take a few moments to be still and think about how awesome He is!

....

 Warm-Up and Stretch

If you're like most Christians, you've been in many church services when the pastor or one of the ministers encouraged you to take a few moments and confess your sins. Usually this type of praying takes place before communion or at a special revival service. Have you ever bowed your head and not really known what to say? Yes, the Bible tells us to confess our sins. In 1 John 1:9, we are told that *"If we confess our sins to Him, He is faithful and just to forgive us our sins and to cleanse us from all unrighteousness."* (NLT)

Most of us know we need to make things right and to start each day with a spiritually clean slate. But, we don't know how to begin. Today's lesson will teach you two practical ways to confess your sins.

All of our sins are forgiven when we are saved. Confession is to cleanse our minds so that we don't feel guilty. Guilty feelings will make us shy away from God, just as we shy away from someone we have wronged. There is something freeing about admitting you have blown it. That's what confession does for us: it frees us and restores us to loving fellowship with God and others.

> **"Create in me a clean heart, O God, and renew a steadfast spirit within me."** Psalm 51:10 (NKJV)

One great way to get your heart right with God is to look to Scripture. God's Word is *"alive and powerful. It is sharper than the sharpest two-edged sword, cutting between soul and spirit, between joint and marrow. It exposes our innermost thoughts and desires."* *(Hebrews 4:12)* (Paraphrased from NLT)

Begin with prayer using this Scripture verse, *"Create in me a clean heart, O God, and renew a steadfast spirit within me." Psalm 51:10 (NKJV)*

Open your Bible to Psalm 51. This is a great chapter to pray out loud to God when you want to make your heart right with God. Psalm 51 is actually David's prayer after Nathan the prophet had come to him regarding his sin with Bathsheba. David was very broken and honest about his feelings and his failures. He had committed adultery with another man's wife, Bathsheba, and had her husband murdered on the battlefield. For a season, David had hidden his sin and tried to go on with life. But, God sent Nathan to force him to deal with his sin. (See 2 Samuel chapters 11 and 12.)

Psalm 51 is his prayer in response to Nathan's confrontation. It's also a great prayer response for us to pray when we have sinned against God and other people.

 Exercise Your Spiritual Muscles

Read Psalm 51:1-19 silently.

Then, read verses 1-15 aloud slowly.

Ask God to show you anything that you need to make right with Him.

> "Don't keep looking at my sins. Remove the stain of my guilt. Create in me a clean heart, O God. Renew a right spirit within me." Psalm 51:9-10 (NLT)

Be still for a few moments, allowing His Word and His Spirit to penetrate your heart.

Now write down every *specific sin* that God shows in the space below. You do not have to make any up. If you're like me, you'll have many things to confess to the Lord. I have found God to be very clear and specific in revealing sins. (You can use a sheet of paper if you'd rather not write your sins in the book.)

Prayer Hint—sins can be actions, reactions, thoughts, ideas, fantasies, or not doing something we could have done or should have done. For example, you might write down things like... lost temper with kids, gave my spouse the cold shoulder, ate way too much, thought some mean thoughts about someone else, etc...

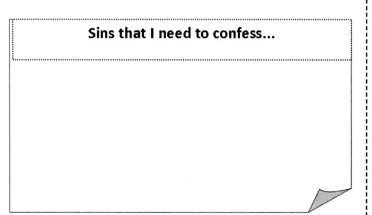

Sins that I need to confess...

After you have written down everything that God brings to mind, go back over each sin and tell God you are sorry for this action or reaction or attitude. Talk these issues over with Him OUT LOUD if possible.

Conclude your time of prayer by looking at 1 John 1:9. Thank God for His forgiveness and cleansing.

One alternative suggestion when confessing in prayer... try writing down your sins on a scrap paper, confessing them, and then tearing up the scrap paper when you have made these things right with God. You can burn the paper, shred it, or stomp on it if you'd like.

Look back over today's lesson and choose one verse that you'd like to carry with you today.

 Jot down your verse in the margin.

> "The LORD is merciful and gracious; He is slow to get angry and full of unfailing love. He will not constantly accuse us, nor remain angry forever. He has not punished us for all our sins, nor does He deal with us as we deserve. For His unfailing love toward those who fear Him is as great as the height of the heavens above the earth. He has removed our rebellious acts as far away from us as the east is from the west." Psalm 103:8-12 (NLT)

Read one more short passage before you close your time today. It's written in the text box in the margin. As you read, underline every phrase that you like and appreciate.

<u>Day Three</u> –Praying with Thanksgiving

Warm-Up and Stretch

> "Prayer is the prelude to peace, the prologue to power, the preface to purpose, and the pathway to perfection." *(14,000 Quips & Quotes)*

A few years ago I read a story that really stuck with me. A woman lived in a rental home that she absolutely despised. The carpet was old, dirty, and ragged. The wallpaper was dingy, and the curtains had been hanging up for a few too many years. The house was comfortable enough, but this woman grew more and more discontented with her dwelling place.

After hearing this woman complain for months, a good friend finally said, "Well, at least you have a safe and affordable place to live."

The unhappy tenant soon realized that her rental home might not be so bad after all. She tried a new practice each morning when she got up. She would walk through the house and name every positive thing that she could think of. She began to thank God for having a place to live. She thanked God for heat, air conditioning, and running water. She even began to thank God that she had carpet and linoleum and curtains. Eventually, over time, this lady became contented and happy again with her living situation. Nothing changed structurally or in the décor, but something radically changed in her heart! She learned the secret of a grateful heart! *[14]*

Begin with prayer using this verse, *"We give thanks to You, God; we give thanks to You, for Your name is near. People tell about Your wonderful works." Psalm 75:1 (HCSB)*

Get your Bible and pen, and let's exercise our thankfulness muscles.

 Exercise Your Spiritual Muscles

Today, you will be asked to think about what type of person you are. Take a moment to determine where you fall on each of the scales. Put an "x" on the line nearest the word that describes you "most of the time."

Would you say that you are more of a:

Grateful _____ Complainer

Do you usually see the glass:

Half-full _____ Half-empty

Would you say that you are:

A Delight _____ A Grouch

Close friends would say that you're:

Contented _____ Not Content at all

How'd you do on the scale above? Did you notice any patterns in your answers?

Now, open your Bible to Psalm 136. Pray and ask God to speak to your heart today as you consider your attitude about gratitude.

Read <u>Psalm 136</u> slowly at least one time. Then, as quickly as possible, list 25 things for which you are thankful. List both large and small items.

_____	_____
_____	_____
_____	_____
_____	_____
_____	_____
_____	_____
_____	_____
_____	_____
_____	_____
_____	_____
_____	_____
_____	_____

There are so many things to be thankful for, aren't there? Sometimes we have to write them down so that we are reminded of how great God is and how generous He has been with us. On my list, I included things like: my husband, my children, my parents, our home, our cars, food to eat, air conditioning, money to pay bills, friends, a great church, our ministry, extended family, air to breathe, good health, freedom to worship, and so many other things.

Go back over this list and thank God aloud for each item. Tell Him how much you appreciate Him and His goodness to you. Even if you don't "feel" thankful, express your gratitude anyway!

Close your time by looking back over today's lesson. Choose one verse that you can carry with you today.

Jot down your verse in the margin.

Day Four –Praying for Yourself and Others

 Warm-Up and Stretch

So often, we tell people that we are praying for them or suggest that we will pray for them. But, how do we really do this? It sounds great, but even the heartiest praying souls struggle sometimes to follow through.

Today's exercises will explore two very practical and easy ways that you can pray for other people. You can use these exercises to pray for a group of people or to pray for just one person.

> "You can do more than pray after you have prayed, but you cannot do more than pray until you have prayed."
> John Bunyan

Begin by praying this verse back to the Lord. Ask Him to help you to, *"Pray much for others; plead for God's mercy upon them; give thanks for all He is going to do for them." 1 Timothy 2:1 (TLB)*

Now, try these exercises as your pray today for your family and close friends.

 Exercise Your Spiritual Muscles

My mother, Sarah Maddox, and her friend Patti Webb have written two wonderful little prayer books called *A Woman's*

Garden of Prayer and *A Mother's Garden of Prayer.* In these books, they give great instruction and encouragement on prayer. These ladies have found some wonderful Bible verses and rewritten them into prayers. Two samples are listed.

"Dear, Father God, please strengthen _____
with power through Your Spirit in his (her) inner being.
Fill _____ with the knowledge of
You in all wisdom and spiritual understanding so that
_____ may be fully pleasing to You
and walk worthy of You." (from Colossians 1:9-10)

"Dear Father, I know that You have gone ahead of
_____ to this new location. You
will be with them every moment. You will not fail
_____ or forsake them. I pray that
_____ will not be fearful or dismayed.
Please help me to trust you with their lives. In Jesus'
name. Amen." (from Joshua 1:8) [15]

Now, go back to the samples above, and put in the name of a family member or close friend. Read this prayer aloud as you think about that person. This is a great way to pray for others!

Try changing some Bible verses into prayers of your own. Take your Bible and look each one up. Then, write the verse in the form of a prayer leaving a "name blank" anywhere that you see the words "you" and "yours." Finally, go back and read these words aloud as you think about someone specific.

Matthew 6:31-34

_____

_____

_____

_____

Romans 12:1-2:

_____

_____

When I pray for other people using Bible verses, I feel like I pray more clearly, accurately, and powerfully. My prayers are not aimless or vague, but rather specific and clear.

> "Never let anyone— no matter how smart or impressive— talk you out of thinking huge things about God and His Word!"
> **Beth Moore in**
> *Voices of the Faithful*

Praying Scripture can make a great difference for you as well. As you speak specific Bible verses in your prayers for your family members and friends, I pray that you will be encouraged and strengthened in your prayer life. And, I pray that you will begin to see very specific answers to these Scripture prayers.

You can also use this method of praying Scripture to pray for yourself. Try using a few Scripture verses as you pray. Place your name in the blank below, and read these verses out loud to God. Picture yourself kneeling before God or sitting at His feet as you pray. Picture Him looking into your eyes and patiently waiting to hear what's on your heart.

> *"Be good to your servant _____, that I may live and obey your word. Open my eyes to see wonderful truths in your instruction. Give me understanding, and I will obey your instructions; I will put them into practice with all of my heart. Turn my eyes away from worthless things, and give me life through your word." (Psalm 119:17, 18, 34, 35, 37)*

> *(paraphrase) I ask You, God, to give me spiritual wisdom and insight so that I may grow in my knowledge of You. Flood my heart with light so that I can understand my calling and the hope of my inheritance. Help me to understand the incredible greatness of Your power as I believe You. (Taken from Ephesians 1:15-19)*

Your Turn: Look up <u>Proverbs 3:5-7</u>. Write this passage as a prayer to God putting in "me" and "my" as needed.

_____

_____

_____

Now, go back and read your prayer aloud to the Lord. You've just prayed for yourself!

Praying for yourself and your needs is not a selfish act! It's more an act of survival. If I couldn't talk things over with God and pour out my heart to Him, my life would be so empty. And, so would yours!

> **"Prayer is talking something over with God, rather than trying to talk God out of something."**
> *(14,000 Quips & Quotes)*

When my sweet husband comes through the door at dinner time, I love to hear his voice, hug his neck, and listen to him talk about the events of his day. It's a joy for me to be the one with whom he wants to share the details with! And, our God loves to hear our voices and to hear about the details of our lives. Yes, He already knows everything we are going to share with Him, but He still loves to listen to us and hear our hearts.

Why not close your time today just sharing your heart with your God. Tell Him the details, both good and bad. Write out your prayers in a journal if that helps you to focus. Speak out loud if you can. He is available to you and listening for your voice.

Finally, look back over the lesson and choose one verse that you can carry with you today.

 Jot down your verse in the margin.

Day Five – **Praying by Putting it All Together in Prayer**

....

 Warm-Up and Stretch

This is the last lesson of week three, and today you will put all of these practices of prayer together. Ideally, you will pray through all five of the steps each day. Begin with praise and conclude by praying for yourself.

Start your prayer time by praying this verse to the Lord, *"Blessed are You, O LORD; teach me Your principles." Psalm 119:12 (NLT)*

Many believers have discovered that a prayer journal or notebook can be very helpful. Some people like to write out their prayers. Others use bullet points or little reminders. You may want to purchase or locate a loose-leaf notebook with notebook paper. Or, you may have a bound journal that you'd like to use. Either way, the prayer journal will greatly add to and enhance your prayer life.

> "For You, O LORD, have made me glad by what You have done, I will sing for joy at the works of Your hands." Psalm 92:4 (NASB)

I use a loose-leaf notebook so that I can add paper and move the sheets around as needed. Notebook divider tabs help me to organize my notebook into the basic practices of prayer:

- ~ Praise
- ~ Confession
- ~ Thanksgiving
- ~ Praying for others
- ~ Praying for myself

Here's an example of how my prayer notebook is organized:

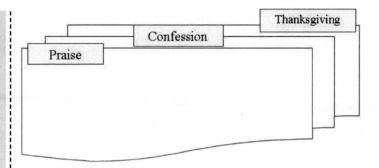

 Exercise Your Spiritual Muscles

Turn to and read <u>Luke 11:1-4</u>. (Paraphrased from NLT) This is the passage often referred to as "The Lord's Prayer." Many churches and denominations recite this prayer aloud in their services. Basically, it is a prayer model that the Lord Jesus gave to His disciples.

Use the passage in Luke to pray through the five areas of prayer. Don't try to make this complicated. Just talk to God. Beside each section, write out a prayer or some bullet points.

Look back to Days 1-5 if your mind just goes blank.

<u>Praise</u> – *"Father, may Your name be kept holy. May Your Kingdom come soon."* Now, take a few moments to praise God. Write out your prayers if you'd like.

_____

_____

_____

<u>Confession</u> – *"and forgive us our sins, as we forgive those who sin against us."* Take a few moments and ask God to reveal any sins that you need to confess.

_____

_____

_____

Thanksgiving – Take a few moments and express your gratitude to God.

_____

_____

_____

_____

_____

Praying for Others – Pray for at least 3 people today by name. Use one of the Day 4 ideas to help you. Write down the names of those for whom you are praying, and write out your prayer (if desired).

_____

_____

_____

_____

Praying for yourself – *"Give us each day the food we need, and don't let us yield to temptation."*

Spend a few moments praying for yourself.

Read Luke 11:2-4 and rewrite it into a prayer for yourself. It's written in the margin for your convenience. But, you will do your writing on the following page.

Now rewrite Luke 11:2-4 into a prayer for yourself. You probably know these verses by heart!

"And He said to them, when you pray, say: 'Father, hallowed be Thy name. Thy kingdom come. Give us each day our daily bread. And forgive us our sins, for we ourselves also forgive everyone who is indebted to us. And lead us not into temptation.'"
Luke 11:2-4 (NASB)

_____

_____

You've done it! You've just completed a prayer exercise! Why not make this type of prayer part of your normal routine each day! There's no magic formula, but this type of a routine can help you establish the regular habit of prayer.

Now go back over today's lesson and choose one verse to carry with you today.

 Jot down your verse in the margin.

Exercise tip of the week

"Prayer is not a substitute for working, thinking, watching, suffering or giving; prayer is a support for all other efforts." George Butrick

Reviewing what we've learned

First...	*Second...*
Start your prayers with praise. Tell God how awesome He is and how great you think He is!	Write out your specific sins and confess them to God. Do this every day to keep a clean slate.

Third...	*Fourth...*
Take time to thank God for all of the small and large gifts He has given to you and your family.	Pray for others and for yourself using Bible verses. Insert your name and other's names into these verses.

Last...

Organize your prayer times by using a notebook. Try to pray through all four of the prayer aspects each day.

CHAPTER 4

What Might Happen If I Anticipate Answers as I Pray?

W hen my daughter was fourteen, she and I had an amazing discussion about answers to prayer. She asked some great questions like, *"Why does God do things like He does? Does He really hear me when I pray? Why does He answer some of my prayers and not all of them?"* We talked for a long time about her questions, and I encouraged her for her honesty and openness.

Maybe you too have wondered why God does things like He does them. Maybe you've also wondered if He is listening to you and answering your prayers. Most of us have asked questions like these. We get into strange situations, and we wonder if God has gotten too busy to bother with us. We question Him and doubt that He hears us.

> **Maybe you too have wondered why God does things like He does them.**

This chapter will address two main questions as we think further about our personal prayer life. As we think about prayer for a second week, we will ask and answer some tough questions. I may not address your exact question, but I hope to address the two main questions that impact our personal prayer lives.

The first question so many believers ask is simply this: Does God really answer prayer? In this year, in your life, in your neighborhood, in your home, in your church, in your family, in your workplace; does our Father God truly hear us and respond to our prayers?

Absolutely yes! God answers prayer!

Sometimes, much to our pleasure, He answers our prayers with a resounding, "YES!" We ask, and He does it. We pray, and we see immediate results. The check comes in the mail, the house sells, the job offer is made, the baby is born, or some other wonderful answer to prayer occurs. When this happens, most of us are so grateful and so glad we serve a God who answers prayer.

> Sometimes, much to our pleasure, He answers our prayers with a resounding, "YES!"

Elijah was a man in the Bible who also enjoyed some very definite answers to prayer. He prayed earnestly, and God answered from heaven. Check out his testimony in James 5:17-18 in the Amplified Bible, *"Elijah was a human being with a nature such as we have [with feelings, affections, and a constitution like ours]; and he prayed earnestly for it not to rain, and no rain fell on the earth for three years and six months. And [then] he prayed again and the heavens supplied rain and the land produced its crops [as usual]."*

Elijah prayed for the rains to stop and they did. Then, he asked God to send rain, and He did. The Bible tells us in James 5:16 in the Amplified Bible that, *"The earnest (heartfelt, continued) prayer of a righteous man makes tremendous power available [dynamic in its working]."* When we confess our sins and pray heartfelt prayers, God does answer. And, often He answers with an immediate "YES!"

Think about this for a minute…

- Do you and I really trust God to answer our personal prayers?
- Have you prayed and had the Lord answer your prayers with a very obvious "YES!"?

- Do you trust Him more when He answers with a resounding "YES!"?

A few years ago, my husband and I felt like God was leading us to move our children from one school to another. After much prayer, talking with trusted friends, and talking to our children; we started looking at new schools. We found a Christian school that we felt would be ideal for our two children to attend. The only problem was the matter of costly tuition.

> Do you and I really trust God to answer our personal prayers?

It became obvious that in order for the kids to attend this new school, I would need to go back into the classroom to work as a teacher. It had been over 10 years since I had been a classroom teacher. So, I dusted off my transcripts, credentials, and such and applied for a teaching job. Strangely, I only applied at one school, for one grade, for two subjects. On my application, I stated that I would like to teach 6th graders English and Bible.

Then, we waited and prayed, uncertain of what would happen next. About a month after turning in my one application, I got a phone call. Miraculously, I was offered the exact job I had applied for – teaching 6th grade English and Bible. There was no doubt in our minds that God had provided this exact job at this exact moment. He had very clearly and precisely answered our prayers!

I remember another occasion when God very clearly answered our prayers for one of our children. At the time, I was praying in my home with a group of ladies called "Moms in Touch." We would meet weekly to pray by name for our school, our children, and our teachers. It was an amazing experience and a group I loved praying with.

One particular morning, we were praying for a bully, a little girl, who was badgering my son to death. He was in the fourth grade, and this girl made his life miserable. She called him names, teased him, and just bugged him constantly. I had met with the teacher, but nothing had helped, so we took the matter to God praying for my son and that little girl by name.

One of the moms became very passionate in praying for the situation that day. She asked God to silence that little girl and to not allow her to say one unkind thing to my son all day long. She earnestly petitioned God to intervene on my son's behalf.

> "Save your fear for God, who holds your entire life - body and soul - in His hands. What's the price of two or three pet canaries? Some loose change, right? But God never overlooks a single one. And He pays even greater attention to you, down to the last detail - even numbering the hairs on your head! So don't be intimidated by all this bully talk. You're worth more than a million canaries." Luke 12:5-7
> *(The Message)*

That afternoon, as he came in from school and we began to talk, I asked him how his day went. After sharing some of the basic, daily information; he mentioned that a really strange thing had happened at school. The little girl who regularly tormented him had laryngitis that day at school, and she couldn't speak. She could not utter one insult at him all day long. My sweet "Moms in Touch" friend's prayers had been immediately answered.

Please understand I am not encouraging anyone to pray for another person's illness, but I do truly believe that God used the prayers and the faith of my friend who prayed protection on my child. And, He can and will do the same thing in your life. God does care and He does answer our prayers. Even the smallest things to us matter to our big God. We may not think He would care about the minutia of our lives, but He does.

In Luke 12:5-7, Jesus encouraged the people with these words, *"Save your fear for God, who holds your entire life - body and soul - in His hands. What's the price of two or three pet canaries? Some loose change, right? But God never overlooks a single one. And He pays even greater attention to you, down to the last detail - even numbering the hairs on your head! So don't be intimidated by all this bully talk. You're worth more than a million canaries." (The Message)*

God does care down to the last detail for you and for me. I saw this illustrated so clearly in the life of my dear friend Jennifer.

Jennifer and her husband James were in seminary preparing for the ministry. They lived on an extremely tight budget with very little to spare. Wisely, they relied on God to provide for their needs. Not desiring to go into debt, they would pray and wait for God to take care of them.

Jennifer shared on one occasion about God paying attention and taking care of them down to the last detail. One afternoon, she opened her cabinets to find only a can of tuna, a can of little, green peas, and a box of macaroni and cheese. She sighed and then prayed, asking God to give her butter for the mac and cheese. She could make tuna patties, peas, and mac and cheese if she only had some butter. A few minutes later, her doorbell rang. At the door stood one of her good friends returning a hair dryer and holding a 4-pack of butter in the other hand.

Her friend explained, "While I was at the grocery store, I felt like God told me to get you some butter. I don't know why. But, I did it. So, here's your butter." God had specifically provided for the small and seemingly insignificant need of my sweet friend Jennifer. He had sent her a gift in the form of butter. *[16]*

> God does answer prayer! And, don't we like it when He does?

God does answer prayer! And, often He answers us immediately with a resounding "YES!" And, don't we like it when He does?

Sometimes, however, God answers our prayers with a very definite "NO!" He doesn't hesitate, stammer, stutter, or delay. He just closes the door tightly. It may even slam in our faces! We may move away from a situation with whiplash because God closed the door so adamantly.

Think about this for a minute...

- Have you prayed and had the Lord answer your prayers with a resounding "NO!"?
- Has the Lord slammed a door in your face?
- Do you trust Him even when He says, "NO!"?

Sometimes, God will answer with a resounding, "NO!" There are times when our great and loving heavenly Father will choose not to give us what we ask for. In His wisdom, He knows that we can't handle it or don't really need that thing or that person in our lives right now. We may not understand some of these negative answers to prayer until we get to heaven.

God answered His only Son with a resounding, "NO!" In the Garden of Gethsemane, Jesus was praying. He knew that He was about to be arrested and taken to the cross. Read the words He spoke in Matthew 26:39 when He was aware of all that was about to occur: *"My Father! If it is possible, let this cup of suffering be taken away from Me. Yet I want Your will, not Mine."* Then, in verse 42, He prays, *"My Father! If this cup cannot be taken away until I drink it, Your will be done." Daniel 10:10-14 (NLT)*

> **There are times when our great and loving heavenly Father will choose not to give us what we ask for.**

Father God could have answered Jesus with, "Sure, I'll let You out of this!" But, God knew what we know—without Jesus' death, burial, and resurrection, there is no hope for us. We needed Jesus to take our place on that cross so that we might be given eternal life. God answered His beloved Son with a "no." Sometimes, He answers us in the same manner.

I like to think of prayer as opened or closed doors. I picture myself walking down a corridor filled with doorways. As I pray, God opens some doors while He closes others. So often I am ultimately grateful for the closed doors. In retrospect, I can see how badly several situations in my life would have turned out if He had granted my requests.

> **Can you look back now and see how God protected you or saved you from a bad situation by closing that door?**

Have you experienced some closed doors in your life also? Maybe a job that you didn't get, a promotion that was given to someone else, a friendship that never materialized, or something else that never worked out? Can you look back now and see how God protected you or saved you from a bad situation by closing that door?

Often, He closes the doors because He wants to open the very best one for us. It's as if He is saying, *"You don't need that one. I've got something so much better for you. It's just down the hallway. Don't give up. You're going to love it!"*

Many years ago, my husband was overlooked for a job promotion. In my humble opinion, he was much more qualified and capable than the gentleman who got the promotion. At the time, it was a hard pill to swallow for both of us. However, within a few months of that closed door, my husband got a phone call offering him an incredible job opportunity with another company. The phone offer was so much better than the job promotion he had been seeking.

If that job promotion had come through, he might not have been as receptive to the phone offer. The closed door had prepared his heart to move in a new direction. The phone offer was ultimately so much more suitable for him and for our entire family. God knew exactly what He was doing as He opened and closed the doors in our job situation. He protected us in His divine wisdom.

> **God also knows exactly what He's doing as He opens and closes the doors in your life!**

God also knows exactly what He's doing as He opens and closes the doors in your life!

Years ago, I was involved in a serious dating relationship with a guy in my church singles group. We had begun to talk about marriage and the future. He was a great guy – caring, compassionate, giving, and very hard working. But, I began to lose my peace about marrying this guy. The longer we dated, the less certain I was that we were to marry.

With much emotion and sadness, we broke up and parted ways. It was one of the hardest things I've ever been through. But, clearly God was closing the door on that relationship. Within a few months, both of us got into relationships with other people. In time, we both married those other people. And, we have both been happily married for almost 20 years.

> "I know what I'm doing. I have it all planned out - plans to take care of you, not abandon you, plans to give you the future you hope for."
> **Jeremiah 29:11**
> *(The Message)*

My family and I bumped into this man recently, and he and his family looked so happy and "perfect" together. I looked at my family and realized how God had closed and opened the relationship doors so perfectly. He had wisely protected and cared for all of us in that situation. Our all-knowing and absolutely perfect God can see and understand things both now and in the future. He knows what is best for each of us.

One of my favorite verses is found in Jeremiah 29:11. *The Message* shares God's words in this way, *"I know what I'm doing. I have it all planned out - plans to take care of you, not abandon you, plans to give you the future you hope for."* God has plans and a purpose for our lives. He knows what He is doing, and He does it well!

Today, be encouraged and thankful for the closed doors. Perhaps, God is asking you to hold on for something so much better that is just around the bend!

At times, God answers with a "yes," at times He answers with a "no." Other times, God answers our prayers with a "wait." This is not a negative answer or a positive answer. Instead, He just delays and makes us wait on Him.

Think about this for a minute…

- Have you prayed and had the Lord answer your prayers with a "WAIT!"?
- Do you trust Him even when He delays His answer?
- Or, do you get quickly discouraged or impatient as you have to wait?

When God answers with, "Wait a minute," it's not the same thing as a "NO!" He often will be asking us to just hold on and give it a little time. I can imagine Him saying, *"The answer is coming. It's on its way. Don't lose heart! Don't give up! I'm working on it, and I'll get it to you very soon."*

When I think of waiting on answered prayer, I think of waiting on fresh, chocolate brownies to cook. You mix the batter, pour them in the casserole dish, put them in the oven, and then you have to wait for them to bake. The brownies start smelling good right away. But, you have to wait for them to cook all the way through.

I find myself putting the toothpick in the brownies as the box instructs only to pull it back out with "chocolate goo" still on it. Finally, after what seems like hours, we get to cool, cut, and eat the brownies.

There have been times, though, that I pulled the brownies out too early, cut them, and served them to my family. They tasted okay, but they were messy, mushy, and not as good as they could have been. When I rush the baking, I am always sorry. I should have waited for the perfectly finished product.

> I can imagine Him saying, "The answer is coming. It's on its way. Don't lose heart! Don't give up! I'm working on it, and I'll get it to you very soon."

Often, our God has us wait on His answer to our prayers. It may be that the answer is not quite "baked." Or, it may be that we are not quite hungry enough. He knows exactly when the timing is perfect. He knows when the answer will taste the sweetest in our mouths.

One great example in the Bible of someone getting a "wait" answer to his prayers is Daniel. In chapter 10 of Daniel, we read an amazing story of Daniel's faith and prayer life. Daniel was in mourning over the condition of the city of Jerusalem.

For three weeks, Daniel prayed, ate plain and simple food, and didn't bathe. On the 24th day of Daniel's praying, God sent an angel to speak to him. *"Just then a hand touched me and lifted me, still trembling, to my hands and knees. And the man said to me, 'O Daniel, greatly loved of God, listen carefully to what I have to say to you. Stand up, for I have been sent to you.' When he said this to me, I stood up, still trembling with fear.*

Then he said, 'Don't be afraid, Daniel. Since the first day you began to pray for understanding and to humble yourself before your God, your request has been heard in heaven. I have come in answer to your prayer. But for twenty-one days the spirit prince of the kingdom of Persia blocked my way. Then Michael, one of the archangels, came to help me, and I left him there with the spirit prince of the kingdom of Persia. Now I am here to explain what will happen to your people in the future, for this vision concerns a time yet to come.' Daniel 10:10-14 (NLT)

> Check out Isaiah 40:31, "But those who wait on the LORD will find new strength. They will fly high on wings like eagles. They will run and not grow weary. They will walk and not faint." (NLT)

From the very first moment Daniel started praying, God heard him. But, the answer was delayed, and Daniel had to wait for 24 days. Sometimes our answers are delayed as well. We pray, and then we wait, and wait, and wait. If we could peel back the layers of the unseen world, we might observe a fight going on over our answer to prayer. Most often, however, we must just trust and wait on our God to answer.

While we wait, why not realize that in actuality, we are not waiting on our answer. Rather, we are waiting on our God. There are so many times in the Bible where we are encouraged to, "Wait on the Lord." Check out Isaiah 40:31, *"But those who wait on the LORD will find new strength. They will fly high on wings like eagles. They will run and not grow weary. They will walk and not faint."* (NLT)

In the Psalms, we are reminded to wait for God to act. Psalm 37:7 simply says, *"Be still in the presence of the LORD, and wait patiently for Him to act. Don't worry about evil people who prosper or fret about their wicked schemes."* (NLT) Psalm 27:14 encourages us to, *"Wait patiently for the LORD. Be brave and courageous. Yes, wait patiently for the LORD."* (NLT)

There are times that God is waiting on us before He can answer our prayers. Have you ever considered that God might be waiting on you to come to Him so that He can provide for you? Consider Isaiah 30:18, *"But the LORD still waits for you to come to Him so He can show you His love and compassion. For the LORD is a faithful God. Blessed are those who wait for Him to help them."* (NLT)

What if God is waiting on us to pray? What if He is waiting on us to give up a pet sin or some harmful habit? What if He is just waiting on us to sit down and be still for a few minutes? What if we are the "hold up," not God?

Recently, my family had been praying about a family financial matter for several months with little to no change. My husband and I both felt that God was leading us to drastically cut our budget. If He was going to bless us financially, we needed to give up some extras and cut back on our spending. We cut everything we could cut, and we made it formal by typing the changes into our budget plan on the computer. The very next day, God sent us some financial help and some relief.

> "But the LORD still waits for you to come to Him so He can show you His love and compassion. For the LORD is a faithful God. Blessed are those who wait for Him to help them."
> Isaiah 30:18 (NLT)

He was waiting to be gracious to us, but we needed to make a few changes before He could bless us! In the Holman Christian Standard Bible, Isaiah 30:18 reads, *"Therefore the Lord is waiting to show you mercy, and is rising up to show you compassion, for the Lord is a just God. Happy are all who wait patiently for Him."* (NLT)

> We can go to Him and we can trust Him to provide for us – even if we have to wait on the answers!

I love the word picture of God rising up to show us compassion. He is standing up tall, ready to pour out His love and goodness to us. We can go to Him and we can trust Him to provide for us – even if we have to wait on the answers!

One last question to consider in this chapter is this: <u>How do I know for sure that God is answering my prayers?</u> There are many answers to this question found in the workbook this week. Over and over, you will be given practical ways to better understand how God answers prayer and to strengthen your prayer life. I highly recommend that you try the exercises in Week Four of the workbook, and I want to highlight a particular exercise that offers a powerful tool for discerning God's will for your life. My husband and I were given this idea by a man we know and love, Reverend Bob Sorrell. For years, he was our Associate Pastor and a great mentor to my husband.

When we were praying about going into full-time ministry, Brother Bob suggested that we pray in a very special way. He shared with us a method that I have simply called the *"Question at the Top of the Page Method."* (See Day 5 for an example of this method.) *[17]*

As we used the *"Question at the Top of the Page Method"* when praying about the ministry, my husband and I would both pray on our own. We would share what God was showing us, and then we'd wait until both of us had a definite answer. When we both had an answer (and that answer was the same), we would proceed.

We have made numerous life-changing decisions using this method, and God has clearly shown us what to do each and every time. I highly recommend praying in this way and asking someone to pray with you. You may want to ask a family member, a close friend, a co-worker, or anyone else that you trust to pray fervently with you.

> **"Call unto Me and I will answer you. I'll tell you marvelous and wondrous things that you could never figure out on your own."**
> **Jeremiah 33:3**
> **(NLT)**

Each time we do this, we don't set a time limit. Instead, we pray daily until we are very clear on God's answer. The words of Jeremiah 33:3 ring so true in our lives, *"Call unto Me and I will answer you. I'll tell you marvelous and wondrous things that you could never figure out on your own."* (NLT) Every time we have called, He has answered us in time and shown us marvelous and wonderful things that we could never figure out on our own. And, He will do the same for you!

Think about this for a minute…

- What if you prayed and anticipated great things?
- What if you began to trust God and step out in faith like you have never done before?

- What might happen?
- Why not go for it?

To sum up Chapter 4:

We can pray anticipating answer to our prayers.			
Sometimes God answers with a "YES!"	Sometimes God answers with a "NO!"	Often He answers with a "WAIT."	When you are uncertain of His answer, try "Question at Top of Page Method."

Moving forward from here...

This week, why don't you try the exercises on the pages that follow this chapter. Try praying with anticipation of God answering your prayers. Invite your heavenly Father to blow you away with Himself. Anticipate amazing things!

STEP FOUR: PRAY & ANTICIPATE ANSWERS

Try it for yourself!

Prayer is such an essential and important practice that we are going to take a second week to think about our prayer lives. After two weeks of practice, my hope is that prayer will be a very normal part of your daily routine. May God give you a heart and a passion to converse with Him!

<u>This week's challenging question</u> –Is prayer becoming a normal and a natural part of your everyday routine?

> **Is prayer becoming a normal and a natural part of your everyday routine?**

Day One –Practicing the Basics of Anticipating Answers with Praise

....

 Warm-Up and Stretch

Begin today asking God to show you how to pray. When Jesus' disciples wanted to know how to pray, they asked the Lord. In Luke 11:1 we are told, *"Once when Jesus had been out praying, one of His disciples came to Him as he finished and said, 'Lord, teach us to pray, just as John taught His disciples.'"* Luke 11:1 (NLT)

Pray using Luke 11:1 in the following paraphrase, *"Lord, teach me to pray. I really desire to learn to pray. So, I ask you to clearly show me how to pray more effectively."*

 Exercise Your Spiritual Muscles

This exercise is called the "Alphabet of Praise."

As you look at each letter of the alphabet, try to come up with at least one character trait for God that begins with the letter. Some letters will be filled with attributes; others may only have one character trait listed. There are some scripture verses listed in the margin in case you need a little help in your brainstorming. (The first letter is completed for you as an example.)

A – **awesome, Abba, able, accepting, alive, advocate**

B – _____

C – _____

D – _____

E – _____

F – _____

G – _____

H – _____

I – _____

J – _____

K – _____

L – _____

M – _____

N – _____

O – _____

P – _____

Q – _____

R – _____

S – _____

T – _____

U – _____

V – _____

W – _____

X – X-tra special, X-tra amazing _____

Y – our yearning, yours and mine _____

Z – our zeal, zealous for us _____

After writing down your ideas, take a few minutes to pray back through the alphabet you've just completed. Express your affection to God using the adjectives and words you've recorded.

This is absolutely one of my favorite ways to praise the Lord. When I start going down the alphabet, thinking on how great God is, I just get blown away with Him! I pray that you will find this exercise to increase your amazement at your great God as well.

I agree with the Psalmist when he says, *"How great is the LORD, and how much we should praise Him." Psalm 48:1 (NLT)*

> "For to us a child is born, to us a son is given, and the government will be on His shoulders. And He will be called Wonderful Counselor, Mighty God, Everlasting Father, and Prince of Peace."
> Isaiah 9:6 (NIV)

> "The LORD is my Strength and my Song; He has become my Victory." Psalm 118:14 (NLT)

Now look back over today's lesson and choose one verse to carry with you today.

 Jot down your verse in the margin.

Day Two – Anticipating Answers through Confession

....

 Warm-Up and Stretch

"How can I know all the sins lurking in my heart? Cleanse me from these hidden faults. Keep me from deliberate sins! Don't let them control me. Then I will be free of guilt and innocent of great sin. May the words of my mouth and the thoughts of my heart be pleasing to You, O LORD, my Rock and my Redeemer." Psalm 19:12-14 (NLT)

Today, we will look at another great way to confess your heart to your heavenly Father. You will be looking up some great verses in God's Word, praying aloud to Him, and then moving on with your day. As we studied in Week Three, confession is never meant to be morbid introspection. Rather, it's a time of just drawing up really close to God and making sure things are "good" and "healthy" between you and your God.

Use this verse to begin your time in prayer, *"Let the words of my mouth and the meditation of my heart be acceptable in Your sight, O Lord, my Strength and my Redeemer." Psalm 19:14 (NKJV)*

 Exercise Your Spiritual Muscles

See <u>Psalm 19:12-14</u> in the space below. Read this passage out loud to the Lord as a prayer.

What does God want to cleanse you from today?

_____

_____

What is "lurking" or "hidden" in your heart that He has revealed to you?

_____

_____

As a young child, my daughter Emily was always nervous that the Grinch was hiding in her closet or under the bed. We often had to look and "check" for the Grinch in case he was lurking in her room. Sometimes, we imagine or allow real "monsters" and "sins" to lurk and hide in the dark places of our hearts. We need to ask God to look around in our hearts for these lurking, hidden issues and problems. He's very good at revealing the "monsters" we need to deal with!

Are there any words or heart attitudes that He wants you to admit to Him?

Now, turn to Psalm 139:23-24. Read this passage out loud as a prayer to God. Then complete the following:

Are you anxious or worried about anything right now?

_____

Will you give this "issue" over to the Lord?

_____

Is there anything God showed you that "offends" Him?

_____

Are you going down the "path" He desires for you to go?

_____

Often, young women will ask me how they can know the right "path" that God has for them to take. More often than not, I encourage them to spend extra time in prayer and in the Word until they have an answer. Be faithful in worship, spend time with godly friends, and listen to positive, Christian music. Also, I give them the verse that's printed in the box below. As you read this verse, underline the words that encourage you.

> **"I will instruct you and teach you in the way you should go; I will counsel you and watch over you." Psalm 32:8 (NIV)**

That's it! It's just the use of Scripture and honest questions. You can use this method anytime you are praying and spending time with the Lord.

Close your time by thanking God for showing you how to make your heart right with Him. Being clean before God is one of the best feelings in the whole world! Enjoy walking close to Him today.

Now go back and scan over today's lesson. Is there one verse that you would like to focus on today?

Jot down your verse in the margin.

Day Three –Anticipating Answers with Thanksgiving

Warm-Up and Stretch

Psalm 100 is a passage I memorized in elementary school during children's Bible drill. These five verses remind us to be thankful and to express our thanks to the Lord.

Today, you will have the chance to make a huge list of things for which you are thankful. We often do not realize how good

God is and how good our lives are until we make a huge list. Without fail, when I am most disheartened and discouraged, I have found making a gratitude list changes my outlook like nothing else I can do. And, praying that list back to God absolutely changes my focus. I can't be grateful and miserable at the same time. It just won't work.

So, start your time by praying these words of gratitude and appreciation to the Lord, *"I will thank You, LORD, with all my heart; I will tell of all the marvelous things You have done."* *Psalm 9:1 (NLT)*

 Exercise Your Spiritual Muscles

Read Psalm 100 two times out loud.

> "Shout with joy to the LORD, O earth! Worship the LORD with gladness. Come before Him, singing with joy. Acknowledge that the LORD is God! He made us, and we are His. We are His people, the sheep of His pasture. Enter His gates with thanksgiving; go into His courts with praise. Give thanks to Him and bless His name. For the LORD is good. His unfailing love continues forever, and His faithfulness continues to each generation." Psalm 100:1-5 (NLT)

Now read verse 4 again. What does this Psalm encourage us to do?

My mother was a real stickler for writing thank you notes to express gratitude. Emails and verbal thanks were not enough. Whenever I received a gift, I was told to handwrite a lengthy thank you note on good stationary. This was just what we mid-southerners did! And so, when I got married, I got to write 1,400 of these lengthy, hand-written thank you notes on good stationery. It took me an entire year to complete all of those wedding thank you notes!

Even today, 17 years later, I am in the habit of hand-writing lengthy thank you notes on nice stationery, and people regularly thank me for my thank you notes. It seems that we live in a day where people just don't express their thanks. Many brides today batch email their wedding thank you notes. Others just send a short little meaningless card of thanks.

We all like to be thanked and appreciated, don't we? I still love to open my mailbox and find a hand-written note in with the bills and sales flyers, don't you? There's just something sweet about receiving a personal note that someone took the time to write, address, stamp, and mail to you!

> **"And you will always give thanks for everything to God the Father in the name of our Lord Jesus Christ."**
> **Ephesians 5:20 (NLT)**

I believe our heavenly Father still likes to receive "personal mail" from us as well. It must warm His heart when we actually take the time to stop and express our gratitude and our thanks.

Let's take a little time today to do just that. Write that personal "thank you note" to God right now. Try the following exercise to help you write your thanks to the Father.

Use the following charts to make a list of the things, people, circumstances, blessings, gifts, and situations for which and in which you are thankful. Start with the easy section, and then move to the hard section.

Some suggestions to get you started…

Easy things might include: Hard things might include:

    Family   Your boss

    Friends   A divorce

Things for which it is _EASY_ to be thankful...	Things for which it is _HARDER_ to be thankful...

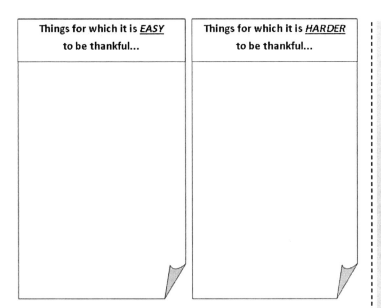

Now, take both lists that you made and read them back as a prayer of thankfulness to God.

Some of the issues you listed may be hard to thank God for. You will be offering a "sacrifice of praise" (as mentioned in Psalm 56:12). Your thanks may be praising the Lord _anyhow_ or praising Him _in spite of_ your circumstances. Just like the unhappy woman who lived in the old, gloomy rental house, you can learn to be content in every situation as your heart and attitude change. (Philippians 4:11). Gratitude jump starts that real heart change.

So, pray! Offer thanksgiving to the Lord for every single thing you wrote down.

Picture this as your personal "thank you note" to your God. He is worthy of our thanks and praise!

Go back over the lesson and select one verse that you can carry with you today.

 Jot down your verse in the margin.

115

Day Four – Anticipating Answers by Praying for Others and for Yourself

....

 Warm-Up and Stretch

"In the morning,
O LORD, you
hear my voice; in
the morning I
lay my requests
before You,
and wait in
expectation."
Psalm 5:3 (NIV)

Another fun and very easy way to pray for others is by praying for them from head to toe. Today you will use a diagram to pray for one or several people. This is a great way to stay focused and to use a visual as you pray. Start by praying this verse to the Lord: *"Allow the Holy Spirit to help me with my daily problems and in my praying. For I don't even know what I should pray for nor how to pray as I should, but the Holy Spirit prays for me with such feeling that it cannot be expressed in words." Romans 8:26-27 (TLB)*

 Exercise Your Spiritual Muscles

Look at the diagram on the next page. List 1-3 people that you will pray for today.

Person 1

_____

Person 2

_____

Person 3

_____

Go from the top of the diagram to the bottom praying for each person. Use the suggestions to help you to know what to pray for. Try to picture this person as you are praying for them. You might think about the color of their eyes as you pray for the things they will see and encounter. You may consider their creative minds as you pray for their thought life. You may think about their courage and strength as you pray for the steps they will take today.

Praying for other people is one of the most incredible things you can do for them! It's as if you are personally ushering them in to the presence of the only One who can actually help them and change things in their lives.

Praying for others is not easy, but it can be the most loving gift that you can give to another person.

Their Mind—thoughts, attitudes, things they focus on...

"Fix your thoughts on what is true and good and right. Think about things that are pure and lovely, and dwell on the fine, good things in others."

Philippians 4:8-9 (TLB)

Their Eyes—That God will help them to look on good things.

"Keep your eyes on Jesus, our leader and instructor."

Hebrews 12:2 (TLB)

Praying for others

Their Lips and tongues—words, reactions, language...

"Don't let your mouth speak dishonestly, and don't let your lips talk deviously."

Proverbs 4:24 (HCSB)

Their Hands—That they will work hard, accomplish good things, and finish what they start.

"And when you draw close to God, God will draw close to you. Wash your hands, you sinners, and let your hearts be filled with God alone to make them pure and true to him."

James 4:8 (TLB)

After you complete this exercise, ask God to reveal any other way that you need to pray for someone today. Jot down your prayer in the space provided below.

> "Prayer is the vehicle we use to transport the loads that weigh heavily on our hearts, leaving them at the foot of the cross. In prayer, we turn to face God as we are, with longing, hunger, and thirst, asking to be filled again."
> **Debra Evans,**
> *Kindred Hearts*

My prayer for _____

_____

_____

_____

_____

_____

_____

Now go back and choose one verse that you will take with you today.

 Jot down your verse in the margin.

Day Five –Anticipating Answers by Praying for Yourself

....

 Warm-Up and Stretch

Sometimes, there is some very specific question that you may have to ask God about.

Begin your study time today by asking for wisdom using the following paraphrased prayer verse. *"Lord, I need wisdom in my life. So, I ask You because You promise to gladly tell me what I need to know. Show me everything that You want me to see." Taken from James 1:5-6 (NLT)*

This next exercise will teach you a great way to present your dilemma to the Lord. Brother Bob Sorrell in Memphis, Tennessee, first shared this idea with my family. We have used it numerous times and through a number of huge life changes and transitions. It has been a huge help to us, and we pray that it will be to you as well. *[17]*

 Exercise Your Spiritual Muscles

This exercise is called the "Question at the Top of the Page Method." A sample is given on the next page.

Look over this exercise. Then, fill out the information directly onto the page. Or, if you'd prefer, make copies of this sheet and use a loose-leaf notebook to make a prayer section of your own. This exercise can be used in so many of your life decisions – major purchases, job changes, ministry opportunities, school choices, and so many other similar choices. It is one of my favorite ways to pray!

<u>Question at the Top of the Page Method</u>: Directions for making the most of this prayer method:

Put the date when you first ask God your question.

Write out your very specific prayer question. If you want a specific answer, you need to ask a very specific question. Otherwise, you may not realize that your prayer has been answered.

Divide your paper into two columns. (The sample on the next page is already divided for you.)

On one side of the page, you will write down all of the Bible verses that God leads you to and gives you as you are praying about this particular question.

On the other side of the page, you will jot down the events that take place, the songs you hear, the conversations you have, and the great things you read as you are praying through this issue.

Watch for God to answer your question. Be looking for Him to speak to you and to show you what He wants you to do. Stay alert to all that is happening around you and your family.

Fill out this page, and pray your question to God. Tell Him what is perplexing you and what is on your heart. Be sure to check back to this page in the future to add notes and to see how God has answered your question.

Question at the Top of the Page Method:

Date question is first asked	Your prayer question:

"Call unto Me and I will answer you. I'll tell you marvelous and wondrous things that you could never figure out on your own." *Jeremiah 33:3*	Events that happen, things people share with you, excerpts from books and sermons, songs that you hear, etc...	Bible verses that God leads you to and gives you as you are praying for an answer to this question...

Choose one verse that really spoke to you and carry it with you today.

 Jot down your verse in the margin.

Exercise tips of the week

~ If you don't know what to praise God for, just go down the alphabet beginning with "A", and praise God for His attributes using the alphabet.

~ Gratitude to the Lord can change our whole outlook on our lives and our hardest situations.

~ When you are trying to find God's answer to something, try using a prayer question.

Reviewing what we've learned

First...

Start your daily prayer time with praise. Tell God how great He is.

Second...

Spend a few moments making your heart right with God through confession.

Third...

Take time to thank God "for" and "in" all things, both good and bad.

Fourth...

Pray for others using the stick figure diagram— start with the head and pray down to the feet.

Last...

Close your time by asking God a prayer question. Seek His wisdom and counsel.

Why Does it Matter that I Take God's Word with Me?

I participated in a wonderful program as a child called *"Children's Bible Drill."* Each year we would practice looking up Bible books and verses as quickly as we could. We'd also memorize about 20 Bible verses and even some passages of the Bible. To this day I can still quote all of those verses because I committed them to memory as a child.

But, do I still take the time to memorize Bible verses and passages today? Not nearly as often. I take the time to learn phone numbers, email addresses, web addresses, and other specific information; but I rarely take the time to commit God's Word to memory. Unfortunately, I am not alone. Most Christian adults do not take much time to memorize Scripture.

Have you seen the "Top 10" lists on television or on the Internet? There are top 10 lists for everything from the *"Top 10 Reasons to Live in New York"* to the *"Top 10 Short-Lived Celebrity Marriages."* When I began to think about the main reasons you and I don't memorize more of God's Word, I came up with two *"Top 6"* lists. The first list is for fun, and the second list is more serious.

The Top 6 Silly Reasons We Don't Memorize God's Word:

6th – My mind is just not what it used to be!

5th – I already know the best verses.

4th – I don't have room in my purse/pocket to carry all of those little Bible memory cards around with me.

3rd – Scotch tape will mess up my mirror (so I can't tape verse cards to my mirror).

2nd – I can't decide which version to use in memorizing.

1st – I had a really good reason, but I forgot it!

Top 6 Real Reasons that We Don't Memorize God's Word:

6th – I don't really know how to do it.

5th – I don't enjoy it – I find it to be boring.

4th – It's hard work!

3rd – It's too time consuming.

2nd – I just don't see the value of memorizing the Bible.

1st – It's not high on my priority list.

So, why should we take the time and effort to memorize Bible verses? Does it really matter that we take God's Word with us? What difference could it make in our lives?

> So, why should we take the time and effort to memorize Bible verses? Does it really matter that we take God's Word with us?

In this chapter, I hope to share some reasons it does matter that you and I put God's Word into our minds constantly. We'll also look at some of the rewards and blessings we will receive if we memorize parts and pieces of the Bible. This material challenges me each time I study and teach it. God often impresses on my heart how important His Word is for my life. I pray that you will be challenged and inspired to give Bible memory more emphasis in your life as well.

Think about this for a minute…

- How many verses could you quote from memory?
- What is one of your favorites? Say it out loud now.
- What is the main reason you don't memorize more of the Bible?
- If you could re-teach yourself to memorize again as an adult, how might you benefit from hiding God's Word in your heart?

Throughout the Bible, we are encouraged to put God's Word into our hearts and minds, to think on it and dwell on it. Joshua 1:8 reminds us, *"Do not let this Book of the Law depart from your mouth; meditate on it day and night, so that you may be careful to do everything written in it. Then you will be prosperous and successful."* (NIV)

See the further encouragement in Psalm 1:1-3, *"Blessed is the man who walks not in the counsel of the ungodly, nor stands in the path of sinners, nor sits in the seat of the scornful; but his delight is in the law of the Lord, and in His law he meditates day and night. He shall be like a tree planted by the rivers of water, that brings forth its fruit in its season, whose leaf also shall not wither; and whatever he does shall prosper."* (NKJV)

> **"Do not let this Book of the Law depart from your mouth; meditate on it day and night, so that you may be careful to do everything written in it. Then you will be prosperous and successful."**
> Joshua 1:8 (NIV)

By focusing intently on the Bible, by putting it in our hearts, we are promised success, prosperity, strength, fruitfulness, and stamina. As we pour our lives into the Word of God, the Bible pours itself into our lives. We can be planted like a grand tree beside rivers of refreshing water. We will bear fruit and stand strong as we make the Bible part of our daily routine.

There are many great men and women of God who also encourage us to put God's Word into our hearts and lives. One such man is evangelist Billy Graham. I read a quote of his that simply states, *"I am convinced that one of the greatest things we can do is to memorize Scripture."*

Another of my favorite authors and pastors is Chuck Swindoll. One of his great quotes on Bible memory is, *"I know of no other single practice in the Christian life more rewarding, practically speaking, than memorizing Scripture… no other single exercise pays greater spiritual dividends."*

Today, I'd like to offer six great reasons for you and me to give Bible memory a try. This is not an exhaustive list, but I think it covers the highlights and offers us insight into the blessings we will receive if we truly commit to learning God's Word.

> **Committing God's Word to memory blesses us with a more powerful prayer life.**

To begin with, committing God's Word to memory blesses us with a <u>more powerful prayer life</u>. The Bible can make our prayers more effective and more impactful. As we read and apply Scripture to our prayer life, we are merely speaking God's Word back to Him.

Think about your children or young family members. Have you ever made a promise to them only to have them use it against you? Maybe you promised to take them for ice cream after the church service. Then, it gets late and you are ready to go home. You tell them that you'll take them for ice cream another time. What will you most likely hear from the back seat? *"But you said…." "But you promised…."*

We can, as God's children, use that same line when we talk to Him: *"But You said so, God!" "You promised us, God, that You would do this thing."*

Let's make this practical. Let's say that you are in financial need right now. There are a plethora of verses where God promised to take care of us. For example, in Matthew 7:7-11 (NLT), Jesus is teaching the people. He shares His heart with them, *"Keep on asking, and you will be given what you ask for. Keep on looking, and you will find. Keep on knocking, and the door will be opened. You parents – if your children ask for a loaf of bread, do you give them a stone instead? Or if they ask for a fish, do you give them a snake? Of course not! If you sinful people know how to give good gifts to your children, how much more will your heavenly Father give good gifts to those who ask Him?"*

As we pray, we can use the words of the verses above in our prayer. We can take Jesus' words and pray them back to Him. You could rewrite the verse into a prayer, *"Jesus, You've said that if we keep on asking, we will receive. You have promised to be the benevolent heavenly Father to us, your children. I need your provision for _____. Without Your help, we will not be able to make it. You have to help us. We so need You to intervene in _____. I am standing on Your Word as I pray."*

This is just one example. As you commit other verses or passages to memory, God will bring them to your mind as you pray. When you are praying for a family member or a friend who needs encouragement, you may think of the actual prayer in Ephesians 3:16-18, *"I pray that from His glorious, unlimited resources He will give you mighty inner strength through His Holy Spirit. And I pray that Christ will be more and more at home in your hearts as you trust in him. May your roots go down deep into the soil of God's marvelous love. And may you have the power to understand, as all God's people should, how wide, how long, how high, and how deep His love really is."* (NLT)

You could turn this passage into a prayer for someone you love by just changing a few words around, *"Lord, I pray that from Your glorious, unlimited resources You will give mighty inner strength to _____ through Your Holy Spirit today. I pray that _____ will open up to You and let you be more and more at home in his/her heart.*

May _____'s roots go down deep into the soil of Your marvelous love. And may _____ have the power to really understand your love – how wide, how long, how high, and how deep it really is."

You have just used the Bible to pray God's words right back to Him. When you and I do this, our prayers are much more

127

powerful and much more likely to be answered! And, when God's Word is stored in our memory, we can do this any time during the day. We can be driving, working in the yard, or taking a walk; God's words can instantly be prayed back to Him. We don't have to go grab a Bible or get to a computer; instead, we can recall a verse that we have locked away in our minds.

<u>Think about this for a minute…</u>

- Have you ever tried praying Bible verses back to God?
- If so, what verse(s) did you use?
- If not, what verse might you try first?

A second great reason to memorize God's Word is to <u>make you a more effective witness for Jesus Christ</u>. The Bible can improve your effectiveness in sharing your faith with other people. As we store it in our minds, we have it ready to use when witnessing opportunities arise.

> **A second great reason to memorize God's Word is to make you a more effective witness for Jesus Christ.**

Years ago, I had an experience where I needed to have the Bible locked in my memory. My next door neighbor, a devout Muslim, asked me to walk with her a couple of mornings a week. We would meet at the corner to walk, me in my gym clothes and her in her tunic and scarf. It must have been quite a sight to the neighbors, two such unlikely friends.

As we walked, we'd talk about our children, our lives, our homes, and so many other things. Eventually, the subject turned to religion. I asked my neighbor to share her faith with me. She talked of her life and what she believed. And then, she invited me to share my faith with her. I told her of God's amazing gift of grace through His Son Jesus Christ. I shared Bible verses and words of hope from the Bible. She was blown away by the concept of grace.

One thing I knew as we talked: I was so glad that I had God's Word in my heart. I was grateful I had committed to memory several Bible verses about God's grace and the gift of salvation. There was no way I could have exercised, talked to her, and carried my Bible all at the same time. My testimony was much more effective because it flowed out of my heart and life – along with God's Word.

What about for you? If you had the chance to begin to share your faith with a neighbor or a co-worker, could you do it without using a tract or a Bible? Have you got enough of God's Word tucked away in your mind that you could lead someone else to Jesus? If not, it's not too late to learn.

> **A third blessing that comes from learning Bible verses is that it gives us a much better outlook on life.**

There are many wonderful programs that teach you to share your faith. With most of these programs, you are asked to learn 5 or 10 Bible verses so that you will be ready to share when given an opportunity. Knowing God's Word also gives us great confidence and assurance as we testify.

In 1 Peter 3:15, we are exhorted to, *"Through thick and thin, keep your hearts at attention, in adoration before Christ, your Master. Be ready to speak up and tell anyone who asks why you're living the way you are, and always with the utmost courtesy."* (The Message) We never know when a great opportunity may arise!

A third blessing that comes from learning Bible verses is that it <u>gives us a much better outlook on life</u>. Having God's Word locked in our hearts has a way of improving our view of ourselves and our lives.

For example, when I don't feel good about the way I look when I stand in front of the mirror, I can say out loud the verse from Psalm 139:14, *"I will give thanks to You, for I am fearfully and wonderfully made; wonderful are Your works, and my soul knows it very well."* (NASB)

The Holman Christian Standard Bible puts it this way: *"For it was You who created my inward parts; You knit me together in my mother's womb. I will praise You, because I have been remarkably and wonderfully made. Your works are wonderful, and I know [this] very well."*

When you and I look into the mirror each morning with God's Word in our hearts, we can call to mind those verses that encourage us. We can use the Bible to give us a better outlook and perspective on those wrinkles or extra pounds, or that blemish that just won't go away. Somehow, when we know how precious we are to Him, those imperfections don't seem so important.

> **Memorizing Scripture can also give us a better perspective when we are making hard decisions.**

Memorizing Scripture can also give us a better perspective when we are making hard decisions. As we think through the alternatives of a certain situation, we can recall verses like 2 Chronicles 20:12, *"Neither know we what to do; but our eyes are upon Thee."* (KJV) Or, we can remind ourselves of Philippians 2:13, *"For it is God who is at work in you, both to will and to work for His good pleasure."* (NASB)

To improve my outlook and my attitude, I need to look daily into God's Word. Then, I need to put God's Word into my heart so that it will be there when issues arrive and questions come.

A fourth reason for memorizing Bible verses is the fact that the Bible can give us much clearer thinking. God's Word can cut through all of the clutter and cobwebs that fill up our minds. It can improve our focus drastically. Maybe you've seen the commercials on television that advertise for "focus power"? These wonder vitamins pledge to improve clarity and thinking skills. You and I don't need these vitamins nearly as much as we need the Word of God to de-clutter our thinking.

> **A fourth reason for memorizing Bible verses is the fact that the Bible can give us much clearer thinking.**

Hebrews 4:12 makes this so clear. Check out the three different translations below:

"For the word of God is living and powerful, and sharper than any two-edged sword, piercing even to the division of soul and spirit, and of joints and marrow, and is a discerner of the thoughts and intents of the heart." (New King James Bible)

"For the word of God is full of living power. It is sharper than the sharpest knife, cutting deep into our innermost thoughts and desires. It exposes us for what we really are." (New Living Bible)

"God means what he says. What he says goes. His powerful Word is sharp as a surgeon's scalpel, cutting through everything, whether doubt or defense, laying us open to listen and obey." (Message Bible)

The Bible in our minds and hearts can serve as a wonderful "knife" that can easily cut through the confusion and the chaos and make things clear. It's like the expensive kitchen knife and scissors set I received when we first got married. My neighbor across the street had known me most of my life, and she chose to give us this incredible gift of Henckels knives. Those were the sharpest knives and scissors I ever owned. They could cut through anything.

> **A fifth blessing that we receive from memorizing God's Word and taking it with us each day is that of increased personal confidence.**

God's Word is like that fine knife or pair of scissors. As you hold it in your head, heart, and life, you will be able to make more sense of things, be more discerning, see your sin more clearly, and be able to judge better between right and wrong. The Bible is an incredible tool to have at your disposal, ready to pull out and use anytime. By keeping this "tool" locked in your mind, you have ready access 24/7.

A fifth blessing that we receive from memorizing God's Word and taking it with us each day is that of increased personal confidence. The Bible can give you courage when you are afraid, boldness when you are nervous and feeling shy. Scripture in our hearts and minds can embolden us to meet more challenges and try more new things.

Our family has moved quite a bit. With each move, we have had to start over, meet new people, make new friends, and boldly step out into unknown territory. There were times when I would have liked to just stay in one place and relax in my comfort zone, but God hasn't seen fit to allow our family to do that. So, we explore "new galaxies" on a regular basis.

How does the Bible help me in these new places? I have found help in keeping certain Bible verses in the forefront of my mind, ready to use when these new and challenging situations arise. When we walk into a new church, a new school, a new prayer group, or even a new store where we don't know where anything is, I remind myself of one of these "go for it" verses.

> **If you need reassurance and courage and more personal confidence, put more of God's Word into your mind!**

For example, I love Psalm 118:6 which simply says, *"The LORD is for me; I will not fear; what can man (or woman) do to me?"* (NASB) Or, I pull out Isaiah 41:10, *"Don't be afraid, for I am with you. Do not be dismayed, for I am your God. I will strengthen you. I will help you. I will uphold you with My victorious right hand."* (NLT)

The Message shares that same verse this way, *"Don't panic. I'm with you. There's no need to fear for I'm your God. I'll give you strength. I'll help you. I'll hold you steady, keep a firm grip on you."* Constantly reminding myself that God is with me and holding me steady makes our moves and transitions easier. Relying on God's Word hidden in my heart gets me through the rough patches.

I know that the God of the Bible, the Creator of this universe, is able to take care of my family and me. His Word is our best reminder of that. If you need reassurance and courage and more personal confidence, put more of God's Word into your mind!

<u>Think about this for a minute</u>...

- Do you have a favorite Bible verse that you can go to?
- Has this promise gotten you through some rough patches? If so, how?
- Are there some other Bible verses you'd like to commit to memory?

One last blessing that we receive from memorizing Scripture is a <u>much stronger faith</u>. This idea goes along with the previous blessing we discussed – improved confidence. However, this blessing is all about increasing our faith and our view of how big our God is. The more we read, study, and memorize the Bible, the more impressed we become with our God. Our Lord gets bigger and better with each page we read and with each verse we commit to memory.

When we read about God's greatness, we see Him with more awe and respect. When we read about His compassion, we appreciate Him more. As we study about His graciousness, we become more grateful for all that He has done. As we read about His justice, we desire to live more holy lives. Time in His Word changes us. Taking His Word into our minds transforms us.

> One last blessing that we receive from memorizing Scripture is a much stronger faith.

Romans 12:2 gives us more insight on this, *"Do not conform any longer to the pattern of this world, but be transformed by the renewing of your mind. Then you will be able to test and approve what God's will is--His good, pleasing and perfect will."* (NIV) That word for transformed is *"metamorphoo,"* and it literally means to be changed, to have a metamorphosis in your life. God's Word can bring about a complete metamorphosis in our worlds. The power of His Word can totally and radically change the way we think and look at life.

Many people today struggle with addictions, habits, and reoccurring sins that drive them crazy. These struggles may involve something huge or something rather small. They may be private or they may be quite public. No matter the struggle, there is a solution: we get before God and open His Word as often as we possibly can. As we draw up close to Him daily and allow His Word to pour into our lives, we can be changed, transformed, and set free.

I was reading an article recently in one of my husband's ministry magazines. The magazine is called *"Leadership: Real Ministry in a Complex World."* I was struck by an amazing idea in an article by John Burke, pastor of Gateway Church in Austin, Texas. In his article, he suggested something called the "60-60 Experiment." For 60 days, he challenges his flock to stay in constant contact and openness to God. Each church member sets his or her watch to beep every 60 minutes to remind them to keep looking to God all day long. They do this for 60 consecutive days. Over 4,000 people have tried this experiment, and they have seen incredible fruit. *[18]*

What if we were to try such an experiment using God's Word? What if every 60 minutes we were to go over a Bible verse by memory? What if we did this for 60 days? I wonder how many verses we could learn, how much our faith would be increased, and how many bad habits God could begin to break.

> **What if every 60 minutes we were to go over a Bible verse by memory?**

God's Word increases our faith and encourages us as we face temptations each day. The Lord Jesus fought temptation in the wilderness with Scripture, and so can we. When Satan tempted Jesus over the course of 40 days, Jesus just kept coming back with Bible verses He had locked in His mind.

Check out Matthew 4:1-4 (NLT), *"Then Jesus was led out into the wilderness by the Holy Spirit to be tempted there by the Devil. For forty days and forty nights He ate nothing and became very hungry. Then the Devil came and said to him, "If you are the Son of God, change these stones into loaves of bread." But Jesus told him, 'No! The Scriptures say, 'People need more than bread for their life; they must feed on every word of God.'"*

God's Word is amazing, and it's even more amazing when it gets into our hearts and our lives. The Bible powers up our prayer life, makes us more effective in sharing our faith, gives us a better outlook on life, gives us clearer thinking, add more personal confidence, and increases our faith and ability to stand against our enemies.

To sum up Chapter 5:

Why should we memorize God's Word?					
It will make our prayer life more powerful.	Bible memory will make us more effective witnesses.	It will give us a better outlook on life.	Bible memory will enable us to think more clearly.	It will increase our personal confidence.	Our faith will grow stronger.

Moving forward from here...

Why don't you give Bible memory a try this week? Look at Week 5 – Taking God's Word with You. I encourage you to try the exercises that are presented. Each exercise is designed to give you practical and fun ways to put more of God's Word into your mind.

STEP FIVE: TAKE GOD'S WORD WITH YOU

Try it for yourself!

As a very mobile society, we have learned to take so many things with us. We are busy people living fast-paced lives. Most of us don't think much about the fact that we can carry our phones, our music, our food, and our water with us everywhere we go. Most of our parents and grandparents grew up in a day when the computers took up whole rooms, the water came only from the tap or the water fountain, and the phone was plugged in and attached to the wall. Today, however, convenience abounds.

Just as we are able to carry things with such convenience today, we are also able to carry God's Word with us. We don't have to tote a 20-pound Bible everywhere. We can creatively take scripture with us and make it a part of our daily lives. This week's lessons will give you some very practical ways to carry the Bible along with you no matter where you are going.

This week's challenging questions –How do you take God's Word with you when you leave the house? Have you found ways to take it with you to work? To school? To work out? In the car as you run errands?

Day One –Taking God's Word with You by Writing it Down

 Warm-Up and Stretch

As I was growing up, my pastor would often encourage us to take notes and to write down the important things that we heard in the sermon. On numerous occasions he would say, *"The weakest ink is better than the strongest memory."* I don't know if that quote is his, but he made sure it stuck in my mind! *[20]*

Today, we will focus on taking God's Word with us by writing it down. Use the written word to help you to see the Word, remember the Word, read the Word, and learn the Word. You can take the Bible with you by simply writing down a verse or two. Start with a word of prayer, *"Deal bountifully with Your servant, That I may live and keep Your word." Psalm 119:17 (NKJV)*

 Exercise Your Spiritual Muscles

"Thus says the Lord who made it, the Lord who formed it to establish it (the Lord is His name): 'Call to Me, and I will answer you, and show you great and mighty things, which you do not know.'" Jeremiah 33:2-3 (NKJV)

Read <u>Jeremiah 33:2-3</u> on this page.

Now, write the verses out in the margin to help you to memorize them.

Next, choose 4-5 words that really stand out to you in this passage. Jot these words down and tell why they are significant to you.

138

_____	_____
_____	_____
_____	_____
_____	_____

Some of the words you chose might have included: *"the LORD gave," "second message," "the Maker," "remarkable secrets," "what is going to happen,"* and others. The words that stand out to me may not be the same words that catch your attention. I chose some of these words because they made me curious and interested in knowing more. Maybe some of the words you chose related to some issue you are experiencing in your life right now.

Now, take your key words and ideas a step further. Try to come up with the main point of this passage and relate it to your own life. Use the space below to write out these ideas.

What does this passage say to you today? How can you apply these verses to your life right now?

_____

_____

Personally, I love this passage because it reminds me that God knows what next edition in my life is coming. He knows what tomorrow holds, what next week holds, and even what next year holds. He knows who I'll talk to, what I'll eat, where I'll go, and what I'll do even before I do these things. Psalm 139:4 (NIV) reminds us that, *"Before a word is on my tongue You know it completely, O LORD."*

Jeremiah 33:3 encourages me to seek the Lord more and ask for His wisdom since He knows the secrets about the remarkable things that are just around the corner. If He knows what the future holds, then it would make sense for you and me to spend time getting to know Him better.

Write Jeremiah 33:3 down in your agenda, calendar, palm pilot, or notebook to carry with you today. You may want to email it to yourself today. Jot the verse down once more in the space below.

_____

_____

_____

_____

_____

_____

"A Bible in the hand is worth two in the bookcase."
(14,000 Quips & Quotes)

Close your time in prayer today. Ask God to help you to take these verses and the "heart" of these **verses** with you all day long. Try to think back over these verses and this message throughout the day today.

 Jot down your verse in the margin.

Day Two –Taking God's Word with You by Using Visuals and Pictures

....

 Warm-Up and Stretch

Today we will focus on taking the Bible with us by using a great visual technique – pictures. Rather than just relying on words, many of us remember best when we have a picture or a visual to associate with the words. As you read and think on God's Word today, you will also be encouraged to come up with some sort of visual device or picture to assist you.

This method is also a great way to teach children to memorize God's Word. You can teach even the youngest preschoolers by using visuals and pictures.

Begin with a short word of prayer, *"Your testimonies also are my delight and my counselors." Psalm 119:24 (NKJV)*

 Exercise Your Spiritual Muscles

Turn in your Bible to <u>Proverbs</u>. You will be looking at two verses in Proverbs that talk about the tongue. Read <u>Proverbs 15:4 and Proverbs 21:23</u> over twice.

Write these two verses out in the space.

<u>Proverbs 15:4</u>

_____

_____

<u>Proverbs 21:23</u>

_____

_____

Now, read each of these verses in the two different translations listed below.

"The tongue that brings healing is a tree of life, but a deceitful tongue crushes the spirit." Proverbs 15:4 (NIV)	"He who guards his mouth and his tongue keeps himself from calamity." Proverbs 21:23 (NIV)
"Kind words heal and help; cutting words wound and maim." Proverbs 15:4 (MSG)	"Watch your words and hold your tongue; you'll save yourself a lot of grief." Proverbs 21:23 (MSG)

What pictures or visuals could you draw or cut out that might help you to remember these proverbs? Use the space below to draw or paste these pictures or visuals.

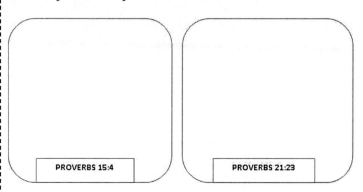

Try to take this picture and these verses with you today in your heart and mind. You may even want to sketch out the visuals or cartoons in your agenda or daily planner to carry with you. Ask God to seal these images into your mind and to give you great wisdom as you use your tongue today!

Choose one of these verses from Proverbs to carry with you today.

 Jot down your verse in the margin.

Day Three –Taking God's Word with You Using Note Cards

 Warm-Up and Stretch

For today, try using this wonderful method for memorizing – note cards. For years people have been using note cards to write down important information and carry it with them.

This method combines visual and written styles of learning to help you put more of God's Word into your heart.

If you do not have any index or note cards, just use copy paper or some other type of paper that you can make into note cards. Post-it notes are always a good idea. The key is to use something that is small and easy to carry along with you. Some stores even sell small index card books that you can purchase and use for scripture memory.

 Exercise Your Spiritual Muscles

Begin by praying and asking God to speak to your heart today as you open His word. Read this verse in prayer to Him, *"I told You my plans, and You answered. Now teach me Your principles. Help me understand the meaning of Your commandments, and I will meditate on Your wonderful miracles." Psalm 119:26-27* (NLT)

Then, look up Isaiah 41 in your Bible. Read verse 10 three times aloud. Consider carefully the words as you are reading them and thinking about them.

> "The weakest ink is better than the best memory." Adrian Rogers [19]

Next, write this verse on two note cards or index cards.

Or, if you are computer savvy, you can type your verse out and print it on some 2x4 shipping labels. You can easily attach these labels to index cards.

Sample card:

> *"Don't be afraid, for I am with you.*
> *Don't be discouraged, for I am your God.*
> *I will strengthen you and help you.*
> *I will hold you up with my victorious right hand."*
> *Isaiah 41:10* (Paraphrased from NLT)

Read the verse out loud twice after you have written it or typed it.

Now, place one card in a very convenient and noticeable place. Maybe you can put it on your bathroom mirror, night stand, refrigerator, or dashboard. Place it where you will see it often.

Place the other card in your purse, pocket, or day planner to carry with you throughout the day. Try to put it in a place where you can easily access it and look at it during the day.

Close your time with the Lord by asking Him to make this verse real to you. Invite Him to speak to your heart all day long as you look to this verse and carry it with you.

This is one of the very best ways to overcome addictions, defeat sin, protect your mind, and give yourself an edge spiritually. You may have never tried anything like this before, but I encourage you to make Scripture note cards a regular part of your life. God's Word can make such a difference in our lives!

I have found some small carrying cases for index cards at the local "mart." You may want to purchase a note card notebook or 2-ring card system. These tools make it easier to carry God's Word with you during the day.

Why don't you write down Isaiah 41:10 and take it with you today.

 Jot down your verse in the margin.

Day Four –Taking God's Word with You by Saying It Aloud and Hearing Yourself Say It

....

 Warm-Up and Stretch

Today, we will try another memorization method that has been used to retain information over the years. This method is the use of the "spoken word." There is something about repeating information out loud that helps many of us memorize more easily. To make this exercise more effective, you can use a tape recorder, a cell phone, or some other recording device.

Pray as you get started using this verse, *"Keep me far from every wrong; help me, undeserving as I am, to obey your laws, for I have chosen to do right. I cling to your commands and follow them as closely as I can. Lord, don't let me make a mess of things." Psalm 119:29-31 (TLB)*

 Exercise Your Spiritual Muscles

Start your exercise time today with prayer. Invite the Lord to show you something amazing as you open His Word and attempt to take it with you throughout your day.

Then, open your Bible to <u>Isaiah 40</u>. Read verses <u>28-31</u> out loud. You will be focusing specifically on verse <u>31 of Isaiah 40</u>. This may be a verse you have read or heard before.

<u>Here are your instructions for today</u>:

Write this verse out one time on an index card or note card. Then, read it over several times. Try to say it out loud 10-15 times in a row.

Take the index card with you and keep saying/reading the verse aloud throughout the day. For fun, call your own cell phone

145

number or answering machine and read the verse in a message to yourself. This will allow you to hear it and to say it.

> "But those who wait on the Lord shall renew their strength; they shall mount up with wings like eagles. They shall run and not be weary. They shall walk and not faint." Isaiah 40:31 (NKJV)

> "Do you not know? Have you not heard? The Everlasting God, the LORD, the Creator of the ends of the earth does not become weary or tired. His understanding is inscrutable. He gives strength to the weary, and to him who lacks might He increases power." Isaiah 40:28-29 (NASB77)

You may also want to call a friend and tell him or her you'd like to share something great. Say the verse aloud to your friend over the phone or in person.

To take this a step further, record yourself saying the verse and play the recording back to yourself during the day.

The beauty of this method is that you employ several different styles of learning. You are not only speaking God's Word, but writing it and hearing it as well. I have found that I learn more and retain the information much longer when I write it down.

Ask God to really impress His words onto your heart as you go through your day today. Why don't you write out Isaiah 40:31 and take it with you today.

 Jot down your verse in the margin.

Day Five – Taking God's Word with You by Using Music and Songs

....

 Warm-Up and Stretch

As we seek to take God's Word with us today, we will try a fun method of memorization. Students have been using this method for years to learn long passages, hard lists, or intricate poetry. Even as preschoolers, my own kids learned lengthy Bible verses using this method.

What is it? It's simply the practice of putting Bible verses to music. Many verses have already been made into songs. Turn on any Christian radio station and you will hear many songs that come straight from the Bible.

The Scripture memory club called "AWANAS" has been using music and little catchy tunes to teach children to memorize God's Word. So, we will try to take advantage of this fun practice for ourselves today. *[20]*

> **Begin today by asking God to enable you to stretch your creative muscles.**

As you start your study time, pray this verse to the Lord, *"Sing a new song to the Lord! Sing it everywhere around the world! Sing out His praises! Bless His name. Each day tell someone that He saves." Psalm 96:1-2 (TLB)*

 Exercise Your Spiritual Muscles

Begin today by asking God to enable you to stretch your creative muscles. You may not feel like much of a musician, but all of us can make a joyful noise to the Lord.

Let's start by looking at a few verses that have already been turned into familiar songs. Maybe you've heard some of these songs or will recognize them from your church or from the radio.

Verse (s) to look up...	One song that comes from that passage...	Heard it?
Psalm 121	"My Help Comes from the Lord" (Brooklyn Tabernacle Choir)	
Isaiah 40:28	"Everlasting God" (Chris Tomlin)	
Psalm 97:9	"He is Exalted" (Twila Paris)	

Now, try your hand at putting a verse with a little song or tune. It doesn't have to be made into a Broadway musical! You just need a little song that you can take along with you today to help you to remember God's Word.

Here are a few verses for you to try. Look up each of these, and then pick the one you'd like to use.

Psalm 27:14   Psalm 36:5-6   Psalm 3:5-6

Jot down the words of the verse you have chosen …

Now, try to come up with a little tune or use a familiar tune and add your verse. Make this work for you. If you can't come up with a song, make up a jingle or some sort of a rap. Use the space below to make song notes or to write your own.

After you come up with your "song," try singing it as you dress, drive to school or work, and go throughout your day. You may even get brave enough to sing it to someone else. I dare you! Ask the Lord to help you as you try to learn His Word today. Invite Him to make it a significant and a very real part of who you are.

Look back over today's lesson and find one verse that you'd like to keep in front of you all day today.

Jot down your verse in the margin.

Exercise tips of the week

~ One of the best ways to learn God's Word is to write it down on note paper or note cards.

~ Putting Bible verses to music can also be a great way to learn God's Word and to keep it in your memory.

~ Having Bible verses locked in our memories can protect us and guard our hearts and minds.

Reviewing what we've learned

First...	*Second...*
Write down the verse or verses you are trying to learn on paper.	Draw pictures, cartoons, or illustrations of the verse (s) you want to learn.

Third...	*Fourth...*
Write the verse on note cards and place the cards all over the place.	Try putting the words to music and making a song from your verse.

Last...

Use any memory trick or method that will help you to store God's Word in your heart.

"The more you know and study God's Word, the firmer the ground upon which you stand will be."
Susan Miller, After the Boxes Are Unpacked

CHAPTER 6

Can I Really Hear God Speak to Me?

*A*s we begin this chapter, you may be wondering – how does this topic fit with the rest of the book? We've been discussing such active topics like having a quiet time, taking part in personal Bible study, praying, looking for answers to prayer, and taking God's Word with you as you go. How does this practice of "listening to God" fit in this book? Is listening to God really an action?

I'll answer with a story. A few years ago, I participated in a book club. Our group would read a new book every month and then get together to discuss the book we'd read. One of the books on the list was, *The Celebration of Discipline* by Richard Foster. The book was not an easy one to read, and many of the ladies just skipped that particular month; however, the book was filled with practical and helpful information on enjoying the Christian life.

> Is listening to God really an action?

One of the chapters that genuinely impacted my life focused on the topic of being more still and quiet. Instead of filling our lives with so much noise, music, conversation, television, and static; what if we were to turn down some of the racket that was clamoring for our attention? What if we were to turn down the volume and become more silent? What might we hear? What might we notice? How might our worlds change? *[21]*

Chapter 6

Think about this for a minute…

- Is your life filled with noise?
- Do you ever just turn off the television or the radio and get quiet?
- How would a little more silence and peace impact your life?
- How might you benefit from a bit of quietness?

As I was writing this chapter and preparing what to share, I had to make a quick run to the store. When I got into my car, I took my own advice and turned off the radio. Alone in the quietness of the car, I just quietly told the Lord that I wanted to be still and hushed enough to hear from Him. After all, I talk to Him, talk about Him, and write about Him. But, do I really ever get still and listen for Him to speak to me personally?

> Is your life filled with noise? How would a little more silence and peace impact your life?

This morning, I did. I took a few deep breaths and told the Lord that I needed to hear from heaven. An issue in our lives was just eating at my heart and stealing all of my joy. I was feeling so out of control! In the stillness of my front seat, I heard these words (not out loud, but very clear), *"You know I love you, don't you?"* All I could do was nod my head in agreement.

Then, as clearly as if God had been sitting in my passenger seat and riding along with me, I heard, *"I've got THIS one! I've got it covered!"* As I sensed God speaking to me, calmness came over my heart. I thought to myself and prayed back to Him, *"Yes, you do have THIS one, and I'm so glad you do. There is nothing at all that I can do to fix this situation. You have to do this, Lord."*

Again, I heard the words in my mind that I believe came from my Lord, *"I've got THIS one!"* At that same instance God brought to mind the many times I had played volleyball with a group of friends from our church. In the game of volleyball, you play with your teammates in a small, enclosed space.

152

Sometimes, you have to call off the other players when you think you have the best shot at hitting the ball.

When you call off another player, you have to yell out, "Mine!" or "I've got this one!" If you don't yell out, you can encounter some pretty wicked collisions and possibly lose points for your entire team. I can testify to the pain of a few of these crashes and to the sadness of a game lost.

In my car today, I sensed God was calling me off the "play." By telling me that He had this one, He also reminded me that I did not and could not get it for Him. This was His "shot" to make, and I was just getting in His way. His reminder of the inner-workings of volleyball helped me to better understand His point to me. He is God; I am not. He is totally and completely able to run this universe and to take care of the burdens of my life. I can trust Him.

> He is God; I am not. He is totally and completely able to run this universe and to take care of the burdens of my life. I can trust Him.

Does God always speak so clearly to me? No. But often I think He could speak to me more if I'd get off the phone, turn off the radio, and listen for Him more readily. Does God want to speak to you? Absolutely! If you will turn down the volume in your life and tune in to hear from Him, I believe that you will hear Him speaking to you.

Samuel heard from God in the Bible in 1 Samuel 3:1-10. Take a moment to read this fascinating story as it's told in *The Message*:

"The boy Samuel was serving God under Eli's direction. This was at a time when the revelation of God was rarely heard or seen. One night Eli was sound asleep (his eyesight was very bad - he could hardly see). It was well before dawn; the sanctuary lamp was still burning. Samuel was still in bed in the Temple of God, where the Chest of God rested. Then God called out, 'Samuel, Samuel!' Then he ran to Eli saying, 'I heard you call. Here I am.' Eli said, 'I didn't call you. Go back to bed.' And so he did. God called again, 'Samuel, Samuel!' Samuel got up and went to Eli, 'I heard you call.

153

Here I am.' (This all happened before Samuel knew God for himself. It was before the revelation of God had been given to him personally.) God called again, 'Samuel!' - the third time! Yet again Samuel got up and went to Eli, 'Yes? I heard you call me. Here I am.' So Eli directed Samuel, 'Go back and lie down. If the voice calls again, say, Speak, God. I'm your servant, ready to listen.' Samuel returned to his bed. Then God came and stood before him exactly as before, calling out, 'Samuel! Samuel!' Samuel answered, 'Speak. I'm your servant, ready to listen.'"

> Our God can still speak clearly to us as well. He may speak through the Bible, He may speak through our pastor, and He may talk to us through music or through a conversation with a friend.

Samuel was hearing voices and he thought it was his boss, Eli. Instead, Almighty God had a personal word for Samuel that night. Samuel heard from God because He got still, quiet, and open to hearing from his Father. Because young Samuel was ready to listen, God spoke clearly to him.

Our God can still speak clearly to us as well. He may speak through the Bible, He may speak through our pastor, and He may talk to us through music or through a conversation with a friend.

He can use quiet impressions, circumstances, and anything else that He wants to use to get our attention. God is speaking, but is anyone listening?

Think about this for a minute…

- Have you ever sensed that God was personally speaking to you? What did He use to communicate – music, a sermon, a friend, His Word, or something else?
- What did you feel God was telling you or showing you?
- Wouldn't you like to hear from Him on a regular basis?

To make this more practical and helpful, I want to encourage you to try some basic practices that will enable you to more clearly hear from your heavenly Father. There is no magic formula to hearing from God. However, there are daily habits we can form that will make it much easier to get a word from heaven.

First, we can hear more clearly from God as we <u>draw up really close to Him daily</u>. James 4:8 simply tells us, *"Draw near to God and He will draw near to you."* (HCSB) In Psalm 73:28, the writer shares this testimony, *"But it is good for me to draw near to God: I have put my trust in the Lord God, that I may declare all thy works."* (KJV)

What does it mean to draw near to God? How do we really do that? We do like my third grade class used to do each afternoon at story time. After lunch each day, I would pull out a favorite chapter book to read to the class. The children would gather around my chair as close as they could get. Some would sit at my feet and a few would stand around me, looking at the book over my shoulders. No matter what we were reading, those kids would draw in as close as they could to hear the story.

We can do the same thing in our spiritual lives. Each day, we can press in close to the Lord as we walk throughout the day. We can imagine Him sitting on His heavenly throne with His loving arms open wide to receive us as we are. Drawing up as close as we can get, we can perch down at His feet and listen to what He is saying. We can imagine the kindness and compassion in His eyes and in His voice.

> We can hear more clearly from God as we draw up really close to Him daily.

In our mind's eye, we can stay pressed in close to our Lord all the time. No, we can't visibly see Him or audibly hear Him, but we can definitely experience Him and enjoy His presence. We can sense His nearness and His peace just as we experience the reality of the wind. We can't see the wind, but we can experience it with all of our senses.

Psalm 73:28 puts it this way, *"But as for me, the nearness of God is my good; I have made the Lord GOD my refuge, that I may tell of all Your works."* (NLT) *The Message* translates the same verse, *"But I'm in the very presence of God - oh, how refreshing it is! I've made Lord God my home. God, I'm telling the world what You do!"* (NLT)

As you and I seek to hear from God, we can invite Him to make us more aware and more alert to His working in and around our lives. Ask Him to open your heart as it has never been opened before to conclusively experience more of Him. Invite Him to show you how refreshing it is to spend time in His presence.

> "But I'm in the very presence of God - oh, how refreshing it is! I've made Lord God my home. God, I'm telling the world what you do!"
> Psalm 73:28
> (The Message)

Another great way to position ourselves to more readily hear from God is to get into His Word. We've talked about this in detail in previous chapters, but it bears mentioning once again in the context of hearing from God. Of all of the ways that God will speak to us personally in this day, He will most often use His Word to speak. On occasion, He will impress something on our hearts or use a song to communicate a message. However, His primary method to deliver messages to our generation is to use the Bible.

Psalm 119 is replete with verses that remind us of the value and importance of God's Word. In verse 18, we read, *"Open my eyes to see the wonderful truth in Your law."* In verse 34, we read, *"Give me understanding and I will obey Your law; I will put it into practice with all of my heart."* (NLT) Often, I will start my devotional time with one or both of these verses. I will read them as a prayer to God for understanding and incredible insights as I read the Bible.

> Another great way to position ourselves to more readily hear from God is to get into His Word.

Whether we read one verse a day, a chapter a day, or even several chapters at a time, God can use His Word to speak to us. He can use our regular, daily Bible study to profoundly impact our lives. By faithfully opening His Book on a daily basis, we give Him the opportunity to use any verse on any day to influence us.

How might this work? What does this really look like?

At this juncture in my life, I am reading through the Psalms a few verses at a time. I usually read only 2-3 verses a day. I write the verses down in my notebook, look carefully at each word, and pray over the message of this small section of Scripture. I invite God to speak to me each morning – to use His Word to communicate truth to my world.

So many mornings, His Word and my life come together. We have a head-on encounter, and I come away changed. For instance, just this week I was reading in Psalm 55:16-17, *"But I will call on God, and He will rescue me. Morning, noon, and night I cry out in my distress, and the Lord hears my voice."* (NLT) All day long, that verse kept coming back to me, urging me to cry out to God at all hours of the day. In the car that afternoon, I heard the words to a song by Third Day reminding me to "Cry Out to Jesus." *[22]*

> Psalm 55:16-17, "But I will call on God, and He will rescue me. Morning, noon, and night I cry out in my distress, and the Lord hears my voice." (NLT)

God had clearly used His Word to speak to me. In my challenging situation, He wanted me to cry out to Him morning, noon, and night. When the pressures of life mounted, He invited me to cry out to Him, and, I did.

He can speak to you through His Word as well. As you are reading, studying, and getting into the Bible, God is able to take the words on the pages and broadcast hope, peace, grace, compassion, forgiveness, wisdom, and whatever else you need into your life. You can have head-on encounters with His Word each day and come away changed.

Think about this for a minute…

- Have you ever been reading the Bible and felt like a verse just jumped off the page to speak to you?
- What verse was it? Why did it affect you as it did?
- How might your life be different if you had regular encounters with God through His Word?

If we want to more readily hear from God, we must also <u>take the time to get our hearts right with Him</u>. Just as we physically take the time to get clean each day, we need to allow God the

Chapter 6

157

chance to spiritually wash us each day. James 4:8-10 expresses it this way, *"Draw close to God, and God will draw close to you. Wash your hands, you sinners; purify your hearts, you hypocrites. Let there be tears for the wrong things you have done. Let there be sorrow and deep grief. Let there be sadness instead of laughter, and gloom instead of joy."* (NLT)

I'd like to suggest an activity that I use often when praying about my sin. I have found this practice to be helpful in keeping me focused and in naming specific sins.

> **If we want to more readily hear from God, we must also take the time to get our hearts right with Him.**

I will tear a piece of notebook paper into 8-10 pieces or use a sticky note pad if one is handy. Then, I ask God to help me to list those attitudes, actions, reactions, and other sins that I need to confess. I write each item on one of the small pieces of paper until I have exhausted my list. On certain days, I need a big stack of paper!

After writing everything on paper, I take each sin and confess it to God. I tell Him I'm sorry and invite Him to cleanse me from this sin. When I've confessed the stack of papers, I wad them up or tear them into bits and recite 1 John 1:9, *"But if we confess our sins to Him, He is faithful and just to forgive us and to cleanse us from every wrong."* (NLT)

After completing this activity, I thank God for forgiving me and know that I am cleansed and ready to more clearly hear from God. Confession is not the time to dream up all of the horrible things you've ever done. Instead, confession is simply agreeing with God over what needs to change in my life. Then, I make it right and invite Him to change that thing, that habit, or that attitude.

For you to hear from God, you will need to agree with Him over what needs to change in your life as well. Once He shows you what He wants to change, give it to Him, confess it, and allow Him to make the needed adjustments in your life. He wants to speak to you and to me, but often our sin gets in the way. Once we allow Him to cleanse us from all of our sin, we can more freely encounter Him.

It's like taking your car to the instant oil change shop. You drive your car in to the shop with a canister filled with mucky, dirty oil. The mechanic climbs underneath your car, loosens some valve, and drains all of that filthy oil out of your car. Once the old oil is gone, another mechanic can refill your oil canister with fresh, clean oil that will enable your car to successfully travel another 3,000 miles. You drive away knowing you'll be back again soon to do it all over again.

Confession is like that oil change. It needs to happen regularly if our lives are going to run smoothly. Dirt and muck gather in the canisters of our hearts and begin to impact how well we are running. We need to go to our heavenly "Mechanic" and allow Him to drain out the filth and fill us again with His fresh, clean oil.

Think about this for a minute…

- Have you been in to the "shop" lately for an oil change?
- Does God need to drain out anything in your life right now?
- Would you like for Him to fill you again with fresh, clean oil?

I love the way *The Message* relates the heart of David as he confessed his sins in Psalm 51:1-12:

"Generous in love - God, give grace! Huge in mercy - wipe out my bad record. Scrub away my guilt, soak out my sins in Your laundry. I know how bad I've been; my sins are staring me down. You're the One I've violated, and You've seen it all, seen the full extent of my evil. You have all the facts before you; whatever You decide about me is fair. I've been out of step with You for a long time, in the wrong since before I was born. What You're after is truth from the inside out. Enter me, then; conceive a new, true life."

Soak me in Your laundry and I'll come out clean, scrub me and I'll have a snow-white life. Tune me in to foot-tapping songs, set these once-broken bones to dancing. Don't look too close for

> "Generous in love - God, give grace! Huge in mercy - wipe out my bad record. Scrub away my guilt, soak out my sins in Your laundry."
> Psalm 51:1-2
> *(The Message)*

blemishes, give me a clean bill of health. God, make a fresh start in me, shape a Genesis week from the chaos of my life. Don't throw me out with the trash, or fail to breathe holiness in me. Bring me back from gray exile, put a fresh wind in my sails!"

Beyond confession, we can also hear from God by <u>putting our senses on high alert</u>. We can follow the instruction of Hebrews 5:14, *"But solid food is for the mature, who because of practice have their senses trained to discern good and evil."* (NASB) The Bible encourages us to train our organ of perception, our judgment, and our senses to be discerning. We are to be aware of what is going on around us, alert to the work of God in our lives.

If we want to hear from Him, we have to be sensitive with our organs of perception. We have to behave like my precious dog Daisy. Daisy is in tune with our family. She regularly utilizes all of her organs of perception to keep up with our whereabouts. For most of her life, Daisy has lived outside in our back yard. Living in the country, Daisy could safely and happily enjoy the peace and tranquility of the shade trees behind our house.

However, she always stayed alert to danger and aware of all that was going on around her. When we'd return from a trip to church or the store, Daisy would perk up her ears and start staring at the garage door, waiting for it to open. We could be a block away, but when she heard that door open, she was at full attention. As we'd walk through the house to come and greet her, she would stand at attention, waiting for us to open the back door and call her.

> Beyond confession, we can also hear from God by putting our senses on high alert.

Her tail would begin to wag, and her ears stuck straight up at attention; she had her senses trained to discern when we were home. If we made a detour on the way to the back yard, her head would turn and follow us to the other rooms of the house. She was intently watching and waiting for us to head in her direction.

What if we were as intently trained to watch and wait for God to head in our direction? What if we perked up our ears to hear from Him and trained our eyes to fiercely watch for Him? What difference might it make in our lives if we had our senses trained to discern good from evil?

Another key ingredient to hearing from God is to do all that we know to do with what He has already told us to do. Most of us have received marching orders from our Lord. He's clearly shown us someone we need to reach out to, a project we need to complete, or a ministry for which we need to volunteer. Have we done those things yet? If not, maybe that's what He is waiting for. If we do what He has already shown us to do, then He can give us further instructions.

If you are a parent, you understand how this works. You ask your children to complete a task or a chore. Often, our kids get distracted and never do what we ask them to do. Then, they come to you wanting something else. You have to ask them to first complete the original task or chore, and then you can help them with the next item on their agenda.

God doesn't get in a hurry. He patiently waits for us to complete the tasks and the chores He has assigned to us before He assigns new tasks. When we leave things undone, He has to send us back to complete the original chore before He can assign us new tasks.

> God doesn't get in a hurry. He patiently waits for us to complete the tasks and the chores He has assigned to us before He assigns new tasks.

When we get stuck, we may have to ask ourselves, *"Is there something God asked me to do that I haven't finished yet? Could it be that He is waiting on me to obey before He'll move me forward to my next post or job? Did He invite me to be part of something but I refused?"*

Spiritually, we can hear from God more clearly when we do every single thing He has asked us to do. Once we have done this, then we wait for the next set of marching orders.

One final way we can more distinctly hear from our Lord is by seeking out the counsel of a wise and godly friend. Often, we can clarify and make better sense of a matter by talking it over aloud with a trusted mentor or friend. Proverbs 11:14 reminds us, *"Without good direction, people lose their way; the more wise counsel you follow, the better your chances."* (The Message) According to Proverbs 13:10, *"Arrogant know-it-alls stir up discord, but wise men and women listen to each other's counsel."* (The Message)

> We can more distinctly hear from our Lord by seeking out the counsel of a wise and godly friend.

One of my wise counselors is my friend Linda. Linda is my golfing buddy, someone I love to laugh with, and one of my mentors. She is old enough to be my mom, but she is just my older, wiser friend. Linda has lived longer, experienced more, and has insights that I can't see yet. We have spent many mornings on the golf course talking over and solving all of the world's problems. I could trust Linda to lovingly provide me with wise counsel on a regular basis. A little golf was enjoyed too!

Linda is just one of many very precious older women that God has blessed my life with over the years. I am so grateful for those who have taken the time to listen and then to offer good counsel to me. My life is enriched and enhanced because of the valuable advice I was given by these folks.

Think about this for a minute…

- What about in your life – do you have any wise counselors?
- Do you have any men and women who will listen to you and offer valuable advice?
- If not, can you name two or three people you might consider going to for wise counsel?
- If no one comes to mind, pray and ask God to give you at least one wise friend to talk to.

What is your favorite sweet scent? Maybe it's a type of perfume or cologne that you or your spouse wears. Maybe it's a food scent – the smell of fresh cookies baking in the oven. Perhaps it's a scented candle that you like to burn: vanilla or cinnamon or apple cider. Whatever scent you may enjoy, consider the words of Proverbs 27:9, *"The heartfelt counsel of a friend is as sweet as perfume and incense."* (NLT)

To better hear from God, we benefit from time spent talking matters over with a trusted friend. Of course, this person may be your spouse or another family member. But, I want to encourage you to ask God to give you at least one friend outside of your family who you can talk to. So often, a non-family member can stay more objective and give you much more honest feedback and counsel.

We've looked at several practices we can employ to amplify our listening skills: drawing up really close to Jesus, opening His Word, confessing all we know to confess, putting our senses on high alert, doing everything God has already told us to do, and seeking out wise counsel from a trusted friend. Each of these things will help, but the bottom line is this: to hear from God, I must desire to hear from Him! Do you want to hear from God?

Chapter 6

> To better hear from God, we benefit from time spent talking matters over with a trusted friend.

To sum up Chapter 6:

How can we more clearly hear from God?				
1) Draw up really close to Him.	2) Read, study, & memorize God's Word.	3) Get your heart right and clean before Him.	4) Put your senses on "high alert."	5) Seek out the counsel of a wise, goldly friend.

Moving forward from here...

Why don't you try out the "Hear from God" exercises this week? Each lesson is presented in a way that will more practically help you to hear from your Father God. I believe your spiritual hearing will be maximized after a week of homework on this subject!

STEP SIX: HEAR FROM GOD

Try it for yourself!

Have you ever heard someone say *"God spoke to me about this,"* or *"I heard the Lord tell me to do....?"* Does God "speak to people?" If so, what does it sound like?

Maybe you've thought you weren't too spiritual because you've never heard God talk out loud to you.

This week's lessons will focus on this whole idea of how we can listen for God's voice and how we can really hear Him. We'll look in the Bible and discover some practical ways that we can listen to God and hear from Him accurately and clearly.

<u>This week's challenging questions</u> – Have you ever really listened to God? Did you hear Him "speak" to you?

Day One – **Listening to God by Getting Quieter**

....

 Warm-Up and Stretch

If you were to take a tour back through the great stories of the Bible, you would find many men and women who audibly heard God speak. With their physical ears, they hear the voice of God Almighty speak. However, I do not know anyone personally who has heard God speak to them out loud. He does speak and instruct us, but not with an audible voice.

> "Don't ever deprive me of truth, not ever— Your commandments are what I depend on. Oh, I'll guard with my life what You've revealed to me, guard it now, and guard it ever." Psalm 19:43-44 (MSG)

Invite Him to teach you today by praying, *"Don't ever deprive me of truth, not ever— Your commandments are what I depend on. Oh, I'll guard with my life what You've revealed to me, guard it now, and guard it ever." Psalm 19:43-44 (MSG)*

So, how do we hear from Him if He doesn't speak aloud? Let's look at one answer to that question in today's lesson.

 Exercise Your Spiritual Muscles

As you begin to exercise today, take a little self-assessment. Answer these questions very honestly.

1) <u>I would say that my personality is mostly</u>...

    a. Quiet.   b. Somewhat quiet.
    c. Somewhat outgoing. d. Very Loud!

2) <u>My friends and family would most likely call me</u>:

    a. Shy.   b. Reserved.
    c. Talkative.   d. The Life of Party.

3) <u>When I am driving alone in the car, I like to have</u>:

    a. Complete silence.   c. Constant noise of some sort.
    b. A little music or talk. d. The radio on & rattling the windows.

4) <u>True or False</u>: I try to take time each day to think seriously about the major issues going on in my life.

5) <u>True or False</u>: Several times during the day I pray over my decisions, choices, and challenges.

6) <u>True or False</u>: I seek God's wisdom often by looking in His Word, going over verses in my mind, and thinking over what He has been showing me.

So, are you noisy or quiet? Do you take time to think through the issues facing you? Would you say that you are in the habit of just getting still and listening for God to speak?

The first step toward really hearing from God is learning to be still. We can't hear from God and know His will for our lives if we are always going 90 mph with the radio blaring full blast. If we truly want to hear from our God, we have to slow down and turn down the volume.

Let's see what the Bible has to say about getting still and being quiet. Check out the following verses, and make notes in the space provided.

Verses to Check Out	What Does it Say?	Do I Ever do This?
Psalm 46:10		
Proverbs 14:30		
Isaiah 30:15		
1 Timothy 2:1-4		

167

One other verse that encourages us to be still and think through things is found in Luke. Mary has just given birth to Jesus, the Savior of the world. The shepherds have just seen the little baby, and they had left rejoicing and telling everyone about Jesus. But the Bible tells us in Luke 2:19 that *"Mary kept all these things in her heart and thought about them often."* (Paraphrased from NLT)

Another translation says that she "pondered these things in her heart." Wouldn't we be wiser people if we took the time to ponder a little more?

In my own life, I have found that I handle things so much better if I take some time daily to pray, to reflect, to think things over, and to ponder a bit more. When I rush around, make quick decisions, and talk without thinking things over, I almost always make mistakes and misspeak. But, when I practice stillness and quietness, I usually am so much wiser with my words and with my decisions. In the quietness, I believe God "speaks" to me and gives me direction for my life.

> **"Be still, and know that I am God; I will be exalted among the nations, I will be exalted in the earth."**
> **Psalm 46:10**
> **(NIV)**

I heard a friend share that she controls her spending by literally freezing her credit cards. She puts each card in a dish of water, and places it in the freezer. When she wants to make a purchase with one of the cards, she sets the frozen mass on her kitchen counter. She allows the ice to thaw completely before removing the credit card. This usually takes several hours. If she still wants to make the purchase after the thawing is complete, then she will do so. Most of the time, however, she has reconsidered her purchase while waiting for the ice to melt. This process has drastically trimmed her spending.

Maybe our careless talking, mistakes, and problems would decrease if we "froze" some of our words and thought about them for awhile. Maybe a little quietness and stillness would help us exercise more self-control and wisdom. Possibly, God can't speak to us because there's too much noise and clutter in our lives. He wants to lead us, but He won't shout above the frenzy.

Noisy Checklist: (Take a few moments and mentally answer these questions or write short answers.)

Is your world too noisy?

- Are you "still" enough to think things over?
- Do you need to make your world a little quieter?
- How might you carve out some time today to ponder and think?
- Could you turn off the radio or TV?
- Could you be quiet while you're getting dressed or driving or working?
- Could you take a walk by yourself?
- Could you close your eyes, take a few deep breaths, and be still?

Pray and ask God to show you what He wants you to do in this area of stillness and quietness. Write down anything He has revealed to you in the space below:

_____

_____

Scan back over today's lesson and find one verse or principle that spoke to you personally.

 Jot down your verse in the margin.

> "Opportunities are often missed because we are broadcasting when we should be listening."
> *(14,000 Quips & Quotes)*

Day Two – Listening to God by Going on a "God Watch"

....

 Warm-Up and Stretch

Yesterday's lesson encouraged us to be quieter and more still in our lives – still enough to think clearly and to hear from God. In our noisy world, it's very hard at times to find that still and quiet place and those still and quiet moments, but it is possible.

Today, we will consider another element of hearing from God. Ask Him to open your heart and speak to you today. Pray this verse as you begin your exercise: *"Open my eyes to see the wonderful truths in Your instructions."* Psalm 119:18 (NLT)

 Exercise Your Spiritual Muscles

> **What if we decided to live each day on a "God Watch," waiting expectantly to see the hand of God personally involved in our lives? How might our lives change?**

Years ago, I read about a man who lived his life on a "God Watch." He would get up each morning expecting to meet with God, and then go throughout his day expecting to see God at work all around him. He was anticipating great things from His God and watching for His mighty hand to work. Knowing that the Divine was alive and well, this man spent his days watching for His God to step in and save the day. *[23]*

Consider the following questions as we start exercising today. Answer these in your heart and mind.

- Do we expect our God to get involved in our lives?
- Do we watch for Him to step in and save the day?
- Are we aware of His involvement in our lives?
- Are we on a "God Watch"?
- Or, do we think of God as some nice gentleman who lives upstairs?
- Do we think our God is sort of uninterested and out of touch?

What if we decided to live each day on a "God Watch," waiting expectantly to see the hand of God personally involved in our lives? How might our lives change? What might we see and hear that we haven't ever seen or heard before?

How might this "searching for God" approach impact your life today?

_____

_____

In his book *Experiencing God*, Henry Blackaby issues a similar challenge. He suggests that we earnestly pray for things, but then we don't watch to see what happens next. It's like we aren't really expecting God to respond to our prayers. Do you expect God to answer your prayers? Do you watch closely for Him in anticipation of what He might do? *[24]*

Let's look at two examples in Scripture of people whose eyes were opened to see God at work. *Choose one* of these passages to read, and make some observation notes in the space provided.

Verses to Check Out	Observations
2 Kings 6:8-23	
John 9:1-25	

Now, read <u>Isaiah 40:21-26</u> in the box below. Paraphrase the main ideas of these verses in the space below.

> *"Do you not know? Have you not heard?*
> *Has it not been told you from the beginning?*
> *Have you not understood since the earth was*
> *founded? He sits enthroned above the circle of*
> *the earth, and its people are like grasshoppers.*
> *He stretches out the heavens like a canopy,*
> *and spreads them out like a tent to live in.*
> *He brings princes to naught and reduces the*
> *rulers of this world to nothing. No sooner*

are they planted, no sooner are they sown, no sooner do they take root in the ground, than he blows on them and they wither, and a whirlwind sweeps them away like chaff. 'To whom will you compare Me? Or who is my equal?' says the Holy One. Lift up your eyes and look to the heavens: Who created all these? He who brings out the starry host one by one, and calls each of them by name. Because of His great power and mighty strength, not one of them is missing." Isaiah 40:21-26 (NIV)

Isaiah 40 paraphrase:

_____

_____

_____

_____

Every time I read this passage in Isaiah, I am reminded of just how amazing and powerful our God is. There is no man, woman, power, or entity on this earth or in our universe that is His equal! He is incredible, and there is none who compares with Him. Verses like these in Isaiah remind me of how small I am and how big and awesome our God is!

> Ask God to amaze you today!

Go back to the verses from Isaiah that are printed in the box above. Circle the words in these verses that most impress you with your God. Close your exercise time today by asking God to amaze you with Himself. Tell Him that you are going to start looking for Him and watching for Him to work. Ask Him to "blow you away" with how great and awesome He is!

Look back over today's lesson and find one verse that you can carry with you today.

Jot down your verse in the margin.

Day Three – Listening to God Through His Word

Warm-Up and Stretch

Growing up in a quiet southern town, we spent a great deal of time playing outside – sometimes very far from home. However, when the sun would start its setting for the night, my mom would start calling us to come home. Although we may have been several houses away, we could usually pick out her voice because we were so familiar with it.

Similarly, we can learn to pick out God's voice when He calls us. Sometimes we might hear His voice speak through a preacher; other times, His voice sings to us through a song.

Invite Him to speak to you today, "Speak, for your servant is listening." 1 Samuel 3:10 (NIV)

Have you heard Him calling out to you lately? Invite Him to speak to you today, *"Speak, for your servant is listening."* 1 Samuel 3:10 (NIV)

Exercise Your Spiritual Muscles

One of the most beloved children's Bible stories is found in 1 Samuel 3:1-10. Turn to this passage and read this wonderful story. Then, answer the questions in the space below.

Where was Samuel when this event took place?

____

About how old was he?

____

Who called out to Samuel as he was sleeping?

_____

Who did Samuel think was calling him?

_____

Go back to verses I Samuel 3:7-8. Why do you think it took Eli so long to realize what was going on?

_____

This is one of my all-time favorite Bible stories. I can just picture young Samuel hearing a voice calling his name in the night. Over and over he would run to Eli's bedside, thinking that Eli was calling his name. But, Eli finally realized that God was calling out to Samuel.

Eli seemed to be unaware of the Lord's leading and His voice. Maybe it was due to his old age, his weakness, or his lack of sensitivity. Although we aren't told specifically, it's likely that Eli the Priest wasn't walking close to the Lord at this point in his life. His sons were wild and unruly, and his love for the Lord had apparently grown dimmer. There may have been some unconfessed sin in his life that was hindering his sensitivity to the voice of the Lord.

We don't know exactly, but we do know he finally figured out that God was calling Samuel by the third time.

How did Samuel respond when he realized God was speaking to him?

_____

_____

Throughout the Bible there are numerous commands and instructions to listen to God and to hear His voice. Often in the Old Testament and several times in the New Testament, God spoke audibly to people. He spoke to them in visions and dreams, He spoke to them through His prophets, and He even sent angels to speak to His people.

Check out a few of these instances in the Bible. Write down something you discover about the way that God speaks to His people:

Psalm 81:8-13

_____

_____

John 10:1-5

_____

_____

As I read the preceding verses, I realize how our God has been speaking since the beginning of time. His desire has been and still is for us to listen and to hear what He has to say. Just as sheep learned to follow their shepherd by the sound of his voice, so also we need to become so familiar to the "voice" of our heavenly Shepherd that we will hear Him when he calls out. As we hear His voice call out, we can more readily follow where He is leading.

> **Our God has been speaking since the beginning of time.**

As you can see, the Bible is chocked full of verses about hearing and listening to God's voice, but how do we really do this? What are some practical ways that God speaks to His children today?

Primarily, God speaks in four ways:

1) Through the Bible — as we read it, study it, hear it, and think on it.

2) Through the Holy Spirit's gentle nudges.

3) Through other believers – pastors, teachers, friends, spouses, and even our children.

175

4) Through other, more abstract means – music, nature, note in the mail, good books, and similar ways.

Have you experienced God speaking to you personally? Complete the self-examination to help you to answer this question.

How has God used the Bible to speak to you?

_____

_____

- Has He reminded you of a favorite verse or passage?
- Has He used a devotional that spoke exactly to your situation?
- As you were completing a Bible study, has He revealed to you some great revelation or guidance?

How has God allowed His Holy Spirit to speak to you?

_____

- Has He nudged you to make a call or send a note to someone?
- Has He woken you up to spend time with Him in the morning?
- Has He poked you during a sermon or Bible lesson and reminded you to pay attention?

How has God used other people to speak His words to you?

_____

- Has a Bible teacher ever taught "the perfect lesson" for your life?
- Has a good friend sent you an email that gave you such hope?
- Has the phone rang at exactly the right moment that you need encouragement?

- Has a mentor or godly person advised you on a situation with great wisdom?

In the space below, share a time when you absolutely knew that God was speaking to you. Be prepared to share it with your discussion group or a trusted friend.

_____

_____

_____

There are a myriad of ways that God can and will speak. He is not limited by any person, place, or thing. Our God is able to get our attention and to tell us what we need to know. There have been times He has used a song on the Christian radio station to just remind me of His love. Other times, the phone has rung or there has been a note on the day I most needed it.

> God is able to get our attention and to tell us what we need to know.

Sometimes I realize that it is God who is speaking. Other times, I think I just dismiss these events as coincidences. But, I'd love to reach the place where I look for, search for, and listen for God all day long. My prayer is to become a lot more like Samuel and a lot less like Eli.

What about you? Do you really want to hear from our God? Do you truly want to see God at work in your life? Then, let Him know! Tell Him how you feel and how you'd like to become more aware and more sensitive to His working and to His voice. Ask Him to make you a "Samuel."

Close your time today by praying young Samuel's prayer: *"Then the LORD came and stood and called as at other times, 'Samuel! Samuel!' And Samuel said, 'Speak, for Your servant is listening.'"* 1 Samuel 3:10 (NASB).

Choose one verse from today's lesson to take with you today.

 Jot down your verse in the margin.

Day Four – Listening to God Through Our Prayers

....

 Warm-Up and Stretch

For several days now, we've been considering some ways that you can listen for God to speak. We've discussed slowing down and quietening your world, looking for God to actually be at work, and listening for Him through His Word, His Spirit, and in so many other ways.

Pray asking God to speak to you, *"Let Your mercies come also to me, O Lord Your salvation according to Your word. So shall I have an answer for him who reproaches me, for I trust in Your word. And take not the word of truth utterly out of my mouth, for I have hoped in Your ordinances."* Psalm 119:41-43 (NKJV)

> He can direct us, encourage us, and lead us through answered and unanswered prayers.

Today, you will consider another way to listen to God. This method involves answered prayer. As we watch God answer our prayers, we are able to see His Hand and hear His voice. He can direct us, encourage us, and lead us through answered and unanswered prayers.

Let's look into this idea a little further.

 Exercise Your Spiritual Muscles

Many times, God has answered my prayers very directly and specifically. A few months ago, I asked God to send my daughter a good friend, and He did. Recently, I asked Him for an older, wiser woman that I could talk to, and He sent Linda into my life. These are some very specific answers to some very specific prayers.

Have you had any specific answers to prayer? Maybe you got the job you prayed for, or you passed the test you were taking, or your child got onto the team he tried out for. Maybe a check came in the mail on the day you needed it most.

On the following lines, write down at least one specific prayer that God has answered for you recently. This can be a large or a seemingly small answer to prayer.

_____

_____

There are other times that God answers my prayer by letting me wait a while longer or with a very specific "ain't gonna happen!" I prayed for a certain amount of money, and God didn't send it. Instead, He taught us to handle our money more wisely and to save up for that item. He taught us to wait rather than immediately answering our prayer for the money.

Has God answered some of your prayers with a resounding "NO!"? Has He turned down some of your requests?

Consider the following questions and jot down your responses.

> "Most of us would be in more trouble than we are if all of our prayers had been answered."
> *(14,000 Quips & Quotes)*

Why do you think God makes us wait sometimes for the answers to our prayers?

_____

_____

Why do you think He sometimes says "NO" to our prayers?

_____

_____

How has God taught you and spoken to you through these various answers to prayer?

_____

_____

Whether our all-wise Father God answers our prayers positively, negatively, or asks us to wait for awhile, He does answer all of our prayers. There have been times when God closed the door right in my face. It hurt because He shut the door so hard and so fast. At the time, I didn't always like it. But, usually months or years later, I could look back and thank God for closing that door. He wisely chose to answer my prayer with a "no" in order to protect me or to give me something much better!

I remember a job "door" slamming in my face. I was certain I was supposed to teach in a certain school, but God had other plans. By closing that first door, He opened a much better one. I got to teach in the most wonderful school with sweet children and parents. It was one of the best teaching experiences I have ever had. There are times I still get to see and interact with those students and their parents. Many have graduated from college, and some have married. As I look back, I can see the handprints of God's plans all over that teaching position. He knew where I needed to be much better than I did. God used the slammed door to usher me into His better plan.

Can you recall a time when God closed a door in your face? Did He open a different door? Can you see the wisdom of His plans yet? Share your thoughts below.

> Can you recall a
> time when God
> closed a door
> in your face?...
> Can you see
> the wisdom of
> His plans yet?

_____

_____

_____

Let's look at some verses in the Bible that talk about prayers and answers to prayer. Look up each of these verses and discover what we can learn through answers to prayer.

Verse(s)   What happened in this verse pertaining to answered prayer?

Genesis 25:21   _____

1 Samuel 1:19-20   _____

2 Samuel 24:25 _____

Psalm 120:1 _____

Daniel 3:16-18 _____

Matthew 26:36-46 _____

As you close your time alone with God today, ask Him to reveal to you some ways that He has taught you and spoken to you through your prayers—those that were answered "yes," "no," and "wait." Share one such time in the space below.

_____

_____

Now, look back over today's lesson. Choose one verse to carry with you throughout the day.

 Jot down your verse in the margin.

Day Five – Listening to God Using Monuments of His Faithfulness

....

Warm-Up and Stretch

For this lesson, we will pick up where we left off yesterday. In yesterday's lesson, we talked about how God speaks to us in the ways that He answers our prayers. He can use both answered prayers and unanswered prayers to lead us and direct us. He can train us and teach us as we watch Him answer our prayers with a "yes," a "no," or a "wait for awhile." We won't always like these answers, but we can certainly learn from them.

> "I cherish Your commandments— oh, how I love them!— relishing every fragment of Your counsel." Psalm 119:47- 48 (MSG)

Pray as you begin using these verses, *"I cherish Your commandments—oh, how I love them!— relishing every fragment of Your counsel."* Psalm 119:47-48 (MSG)

Today, we will carry this idea a little further by thinking about patterns of answered prayer and something my friend Debbie Settle calls "Monuments to God's Faithfulness." Debbie taught me the value of tracking God's faithful hand across the years of our lives. She encouraged me to see that God is always at work in our lives and that He is so good to continue that work year after year. *[25]*

 Exercise Your Spiritual Muscles

Our family likes to do something that may seem a little strange to you: we like to walk through a graveyard and read the tombstones. We do this in the day time, of course, we enjoy reading people's names, their birth dates, and the epitaphs that are carved onto their headstones. These tombstones are really the only reminders of some people's lives. We can learn a little bit about them through these "monuments" that were built just for them.

Similarly, we can "build" monuments to God's faithfulness in our own lives. We can read and remember the many ways that God has worked in the past to protect us and to guide us. As we look back to the past, we can garner much needed hope and encouragement to survive in the present and in the upcoming future.

So, let's take a look first at what the Bible teaches us about making monuments to God's faithfulness. And then, we'll construct some "monuments" of our own. Open to each of these verses in God's Word, and write down one thing you learn about remembrances, monuments, and God's faithfulness.

Verse (s)	What does the verse say about monuments & remembrances?
Exodus 13:1-3	_____
Deuteronomy 7:16-20	_____
Joshua 4:1-9	_____
1 Chronicles 16:12-15	_____
Psalm 77:11-12	_____

Now, let's make this personal and practical. Take a few minutes to think back to some significant moments when you saw God's hand work in your life. Maybe it was when you met your spouse. It could have been when God allowed you to have a baby. Possibly it was when He rescued you from some sort of disaster – physical or emotional.

Stones of remembrance could include…

- Meeting Jesus Christ personally
- Telling someone else about the Lord
- Meeting and marrying spouse
- Having first baby or moving into your first home
- Spending time with an older and wiser mentor
- Going on your first mission trip
- Seeing God really use your life to impact someone else's life
- Attending an Emmaus Walk, Faithwalk, or special retreat

- Anything else of great importance in your spiritual journey and your life

The first stone has been filled in for you. Take the time to fill in at least 5-6 more of these stones of remembrance. Enjoy! This is a wonderful way to look back and see the hand of God at work in your life. I think you will be amazed by what you discover!

Monuments to God's Faithfulness in my Life:

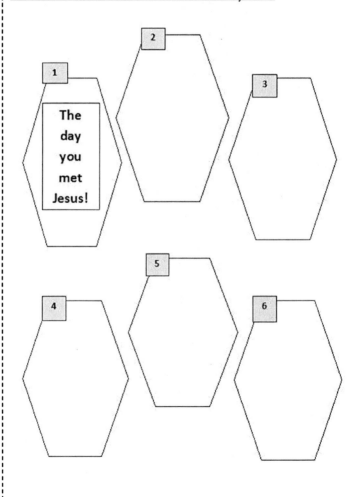

Look back over the monuments to God's faithfulness that you just recorded. Then, answer the following questions:

Can you see any patterns in your life and your walk with God?

_____

_____

How are you encouraged as you look back?

_____

_____

How has God used these monuments to His faithfulness to speak to you?

_____

_____

When I look back and consider these monuments in my own life, I feel so loved by God. I also recognize His hand and His creative touch in my life year after year. These monuments remind me that I am not living life on this planet on my own. I have a divine Creator and Planner close behind the scene looking out for me and taking care of my life. Think about the amazing way that our God can take complete care of my life and totally handle your life and all of our lives at the very same time. Almighty God is able to hold my "world" and this world both perfectly in their places!

> "And I am sure that God, who began the good work within you, will continue His work until it is finally finished on that day when Christ Jesus comes back again."
> Philippians 1:6 (NLT)

As I talked to some of my sweet friends about this particular topic, we discussed the way the Old Testament believers practiced this same exercise. They would literally stack up stones or build a stone altar to help them remember the place and the way God was good to them, then they would typically name the place after a characteristic of God. For example, when Abraham was spared from sacrificing his son Isaac, he named the place *"Jehovah Jireh"* which means, *"the LORD will provide."*

> "Acceptance is taking from God's hand absolutely anything He chooses to give us, looking up into His face in love and trust—even in thanksgiving—and knowing that the confines of the hedge within which He has placed us are good, even perfect, however painful they may be, simply because He Himself has given them."
> Chuck Swindoll, *Swindoll's Ultimate Book of Illustrations and Quotes*

Try this practice yourself. Go back once more to your *"Monuments to God's Faithfulness"* on the preceding page. Beside each of these stones, write down one of God's character traits. For example, next to the stone that represents your salvation, you might put the words "God's mercy and grace." Beside the stone that represents the birth of a child, you may write, "God's goodness." Try to think of at least one characteristic of our awesome God that would apply to each of your life situations.

Close in prayer and thank the Lord for being actively involved in your life. Thank Him for His faithfulness and for taking care of your life with such detail and precision. Thank Him for not being passive and distant. Tell Him how much you appreciate His work and His hand.

Look back over today's lesson and choose one verse that was meaningful to you.

 Jot down your verse in the margin.

Exercise tips of the week

~ Being still and quiet is more a frame of mind than a posture of the body.

~ Go on a big "hunt" for God in your life. Look and listen for Him in everything.

Reviewing what we've learned

First... Get still and quiet if you want to start hearing more from God.	*Second...* Start a "God Watch" looking for God to do something great in your life!
Third... Go to God's Word to get His view and His wisdom on things.	*Fourth...* Pray specifically and look for specific answers to your prayers. Write them down to help you remember.

Last...
Look back to how God has worked in your life in the past. Be encouraged that He still moves!

CHAPTER 7

Help! I'm Tired!

She would usually arrive at the door about 3:30 in the afternoon. She'd have her arms filled with bags of dolls and toys. Her name was Mackenzie, and she was my daughter's best friend in the first and second grades. Mackenzie was a smart, beautiful, feisty little thing that only stood about three feet tall. She and my daughter Emily would spend hours together playing with dolls, miniature furniture, and animals.

In fact, many days the girls would spend hours setting up tiny towns, farms, villages, houses, and families. When they got together, imaginations soared, and pretending kicked into a whole new gear. I have so many sweet memories of listening to those two little girls playing happily for hours at a time.

> Do you ever just want to take your "toys" and go home?

But, every once in awhile, there would be trouble in the house. One or both of the girls would get aggravated with the other, and an argument would ensue. Typically, Mackenzie would start to pack up her things and head for the door. On more than one occasion, I heard her say in her most indignant voice, "I'm taking my toys and going home!" I'd watch her walk home and call her mom to let her know what had happened.

Do you ever feel like my daughter's friend Mackenzie? Do you ever want to take your "toys" and just go home? In other words, do you ever want to quit?

All of us feel like quitting at times! People want to quit their jobs, their workout or diet plans, their marriages, their churches, their friendships, or their ministries. People get weary and people quit.

Think about this for a minute...

- Do you ever feel like taking your toys and going home?
- Have you really wanted to give up on something recently? If so, what was it and why did you want to give up?

All people grow tired at times, and all of us have been tempted to bail out at one point or another in our lives. Did you know that even great Bible men and women felt the same way and wanted to quit at times?

Let's look at one such situation in the Old Testament. Take a moment and read the story that is printed below:

> **Did you know that even great Bible men and women felt the same way and wanted to quit at times?**

"When Ahab got home, he told Jezebel what Elijah had done and that he had slaughtered the prophets of Baal. So Jezebel sent this message to Elijah: 'May the gods also kill me if by this time tomorrow I have failed to take your life like those whom you killed.' Elijah was afraid and fled for his life. He went to Beersheba, a town in Judah, and he left his servant there. Then he went on alone into the desert, traveling all day. He sat down under a solitary broom tree and prayed that he might die. 'I have had enough, LORD,' he said. 'Take my life, for I am no better than my ancestors.' Then he lay down and slept under the broom tree. But as he was sleeping, an angel touched him and told him, 'Get up and eat!' He looked around and saw some bread baked on hot stones and a jar of water! So he ate and drank and lay down again. Then the angel of the LORD came again and touched him and said, 'Get up and eat some more, for there is a long journey ahead of you.' So he got up and ate and drank, and the food gave him enough strength to travel forty days and forty nights to Mount Sinai, the mountain of God." I Kings 19:1-8 (NLT)

Elijah was an incredible man of God. He was a prayer warrior and a person who had personally experienced God's power in his life. However, he was still just a human being – made of skin and bones just as we are. He had ups and downs just as we do.

In this particular account, we catch Elijah in a dry season in his life – on a down day. Let's look at his story and discover some lessons we can learn from what he went through. Most of the story takes place in the desert under a broom tree. So, this lesson has been called *"Lessons We Can Learn from Time Under a Desert Broom Tree."*

Lesson One: <u>Everyone gets scared and runs away at times (or wants to run away)</u>. Elijah had just been threatened by the wicked Queen Jezebel, and we are told, *"Elijah was afraid and fled for his life."* Do you ever feel afraid? Threatened? Want to get away from it all? You are not alone. All of us get scared and desire to retreat at times.

> Everyone gets scared and runs away at times (or wants to run away).

Lesson Two: <u>All of us get tired and want to quit sometimes!</u> Elijah felt this way in 1 Kings 19:4, *"Then he went on alone into the desert, travelling all day. He sat down under a solitary broom tree and prayed that he might die. 'I have had enough, Lord,' he said. 'Take my life, for I am not better than my ancestors.'"* (NLT) Elijah had enough. He was at the end of his rope, and he wanted God to take his life. The man was in great need of some rest and relaxation, so, he took some time out under a broom tree.

In sports when your team is getting weary and out of breath, what does a good coach do? He or she calls a *"time out."* In music, a great conductor will pause and allow his musicians the chance to catch their breath. On a page of music, it's called a *"rest."* How about in ministry and in church work? What do we call that period of time when we are weary and need a little respite? Can't think of anything either? That's because there are not any planned breaks in church work, at least none that I could find.

I did explore on the Internet to try and find "church time outs" or "church rests" or "church breaks," but I could not find any practices that are regularly encouraged in any of our Protestant denominations. Maybe other religions employ some sort of down time, but in most American churches, we are pretty clueless on this topic.

But, we can allow ourselves time to retreat and recover even if our churches do not. In our own personal lives, we can make allowances for time out anytime and anywhere. It's just a matter of making down time a priority!

> All of us get tired and want to quit sometimes!

So, what might a "Broom Tree" look like in the United States today? If we were to look for a place to go for some regularly scheduled rest and relaxation, where might we go? To take a few moments and refill our tanks, what might we do?

For some of us, a walk outdoors can renew our hearts and put a little bounce back into our steps. For others, we need time with a trusted friend, time to talk, listen, laugh, and enjoy. Some folks retreat to a certain comfortable chair or swing. You may enjoy time getting your nails done or having your hair cut.

Think about this for a minute...

- Do you have a "Broom Tree" place where you can escape and unwind?
- If not, why don't you jot down 3-4 places you might try to make into "Broom Trees"?

> "Broom Tree Moments" are necessary and needed!

Lesson Three: "Broom Tree Moments" are necessary and needed! Elijah had reached his breaking point. He needed some time under that Broom Tree. See his words again in 1 Kings 19:4, *"I have had enough," Lord, he said. "Take my life, for I am no better than my ancestors."* (NLT)

When we push the parameters too far, we will burn out! Without rest, we all grow weary. No one can go forever without taking some breaks. In fact, most of us suffer the consequences when we push ourselves too hard and too long.

If I go at life too hard and too long, I usually get physically sick. God has created me in such a way that I need plenty of rest, sleep, good food, exercise, and sweet fellowship with other people in my life. If I don't get all of these things, over time I will get sick. What about in your life? When you push yourself too far and too long, what usually happens to you? Do you get sick, grumpy, angry, moody, weepy, or something else?

Lesson Four: Without "Broom Tree Moments," we will burn out! If we don't take some breaks along the road of life, we will break down. Just as our vehicles cannot go forever without fuel, water, and fresh oil, we cannot go forever without refreshment and refueling.

Elijah needed both in 1 Kings 19:5-6, *"Then he lay down and slept under the broom tree. But as he was sleeping, an angel touched him and told him, 'Get up and eat!' He looked around and saw some bread baked on hot stones and a jar of water! So he ate and drank and lay down again."* (NLT) In Elijah's exhaustion, God sent him hot bread and a big jar of fresh water. He didn't send him another prophet or a sermon or a book. Rather, God used something very practical to restore and renew Elijah's soul.

Our God often does the same thing in our lives. When we are weary and feeling blue, He will send us a sweet note in the mail, or the hug of a friend, or the laughter and kindness of a little child, or even a good night of sleep. What is one practical way God often chooses to restore and refresh your life? What is something He has used to renew you recently?

> **Without "Broom Tree Moments," we will burn out!**

For me, He has been using sweet music to restore my heart in recent days. Whether I've been in my car or at my computer, God has utilized the words and melodies of several inspirational songs lately to cheer and to revive my spirit. As the music plays, fresh life seems to pour over my whole being. I can agree with David in Psalm 23:1-3, *"The LORD is my shepherd; I have*

193

everything I need. He lets me rest in green meadows; He leads me beside peaceful streams. He renews my strength." (NLT)

<u>Lesson Five</u>: <u>God knows what's coming next in our lives, so He uses "Broom Tree Moments" to get us ready for what's ahead.</u> God knew all that was about to take place in Elijah's life; He knew Elijah's future and all of the events that were about to unfold. Time under the Broom Tree was needed and necessary to prepare Elijah for what was ahead.

> **God knows what's coming next in our lives, so He uses "Broom Tree Moments" to get us ready for what's ahead.**

Check out 1 Kings 19:7 where the angel explains this to Elijah, *"Then the angel of the Lord came again and touched him and said, 'Get up and eat some more, for there is a long journey ahead of you.'"* (NLT) Elijah had no idea what was going to happen next, but God made sure he was ready for it anyway.

Our Father God can and will do the same thing for us. If He encourages us to take a seat and rest up, then He knows we are going to need it for all that is ahead in our lives. If He knows what's coming next, then I can trust Him to get me prepared for it. It's not up to me to prepare myself for my unknown future; it's up to Almighty God.

I'm one of those women who has tried her hand at a little coaching over the years, primarily in the sport of basketball. My last few years to coach, I worked with 5th and 6th grade girls. I had the cutest, sweetest bunch of girls on my last team, but we were small and easily overpowered by most other teams. My job was to try to prepare those girls for each upcoming game.

I would watch other teams play, talk to other coaches, and make game plans that would give my team every possibly advantage in each game we played. All my girls had to do was to show up, practice hard, and play together. They didn't have to worry about the next game or the next opponent. That was my job. I was the one ultimately responsible for getting them ready to play each and every game. They just had to look to me and listen to my instructions.

God is like a fabulous coach. He knows who our next opponent is. He knows which team we have to play next week. He knows what we need to do to get ready for the upcoming game. And, He can prepare us if we will just let Him. Our role is to listen to Him and follow His instructions. When those instructions have us sitting on the sidelines, then that's part of His master plan as well.

Lesson Six: When it's time for you to get up and get out there again, He'll get you up and get you going again. When Elijah's respite was over, God let him know. He didn't have to wonder or ask; God got him up. Read 1 Kings 19:7-9 once more, *"Then the angel of the Lord came again and touched him and said, 'Get up and eat some more, for there is a long journey ahead of you.' So he got up and ate and drank, and the food gave him enough strength to travel forty days and forty nights to Mount Sinai, the mountain of God."* (NLT)

God got Elijah up, filled him up with good food, and sent him to the next destination. When it was time to move on, Elijah knew. There was no doubt that his "Broom Tree Moment" was over.

For some of you, this week's lesson has found you weary and in need of some "Broom Tree Moments." I encourage you to take those breaks. Find some places where you can be renewed and refreshed. Allow your Shepherd to lead you beside some quiet "waters" and restore your strength.

For others of you, you need to be encouraged to get out from under the tree and back into the game. You have been resting and soaking in the love of God. He has given you some time to catch your breath. But now, He needs you to get back out there and serve again. You have so much to offer and so much to give. This was only a break, and the break is over!

> When it's time for you to get up and get out there again, He'll get you up and get you going again.

195

To sum up Chapter 7:

Lessons we can learn in times of rest - "Broom Tree Moments".					
All of us get scared & want to run away at times.	Everyone gets tired & wants to quit sometimes.	"Broom Tree Moments" are needed & necessary.	Without rest, we will burn out!	God knows what's coming next, & He uses "Broom Tree Moments" to get us ready.	When it's time for us to get up, God will get us up & get us going again.

Moving forward from here...

This week is the final week for you to work on your own. I want to encourage you to complete all five days of exercises. I'm praying He'll use each day to broaden your view of the amazing things He can do in and through your life.

STEP SEVEN: GET INVOLVED WITH OTHERS

Try it for yourself!

Everything we've studied up until now has been primarily personal and private; however, this last chapter will encourage you to get out there and get involved with other people. For some of you, dealing with other people is easy and a part of what you do; for others, getting involved with other people will challenge you to the very core.

Whether you are shy or very outgoing, this week's studies will challenge you to reflect on your relationships with those who know Christ and with those who do not. We'll begin with the church and end with the world. Invite God to speak to you personally as you complete this last chapter in our study.

<u>This week's challenging questions</u> – In what ways are you allowing God to use you to impact and influence others for His kingdom? How are you allowing God to mentor and encourage you in your spiritual walk through the lives of other believers?

Day One – Getting Involved with Others by Getting Plugged in to a Great Church

 Warm-Up and Stretch

> **"You need the church, the church needs you, and the world needs both."** *(14,000 Quips & Quotes)*

Start your time with prayer, "Father, I desire to *Seek the LORD and His strength; seek His face continually.*" *1 Chronicles 16:11 (NASB)*

To get your spiritual muscles warmed up today, try this self-assessment. Choose all that apply.

1) <u>I go to church primarily</u>... (Circle all that apply)

    a.   For the incredible food and coffee

    b.   For the fellowship and conversations with friends

    c.   For the teaching, preaching, and training I get

    d.   To network and build my business

    e.   Because I feel guilty if I don't go

> **"But while Peter was in prison, the church prayed very earnestly for him."** Acts 12:5 (NLT)

2) <u>I have joined a church and started attending</u>...

    a.   Almost every week

    b.   About twice a month

    c.   Every few weeks or so

3) <u>I haven't joined a church yet because</u>...

a. Not applicable—I have joined!!

b. My spouse won't go with me.

c. I haven't met enough people yet.

d. I don't want to walk down the aisle.

e. I don't want to take that new member class.

f. I plan to, but I just keep putting it off.

4) I think people need a church home primarily for…

    a. Christian friends.

    b. Networking/meeting people.

    c. Growing as a Christian.

    d. Being able to use their spiritual gift.

Why do we need a church home? Why does it matter that we go to church? There are many reasons people choose to get up and go to church each week, and there are many reasons that people choose not to attend a church. Today's exercise will encourage you to think about the benefits of being involved in a growing church and take you to some Scriptures that encourage us to assemble together with other believers.

 Exercise Your Spiritual Muscles

Begin your exercise routine today by filling in the two spaces below. There are no wrong or right answers!

Top Reasons I go to church:

1) _____

2) _____

3) _____

Top Reasons I miss/skip church:

1) _____

2) _____

3) _____

When you invite other people to come to church with you, what do you tell them about your church?

_____

_____

How friendly the people are?

_____

How great the music is?

_____

Let's look into God's word to find out why the early Christians went to church. Check out each of these verses. Then write down one reason the first believers assembled together.

Verse (s)   According to this passage, what is one
                   reason the early Christians met?

Acts 9:31   _____

Acts 11:19-26   _____

Acts 12:5-17   _____

Acts 14:21-28   _____

When you look at some of the reasons the early church met, you find a myriad of activities that encouraged their gathering together. Often, they met to pray for one of their leaders who was in prison. Other times, they met to share what God was doing in their lives. Sometimes, they met for worship, for teaching, for Bible reading, or to hear a testimony.

We are the same way today, aren't we? We meet together for Bible study, for prayer, and for teaching, but we also get together when there is a need or an emergency. Many Christians will get with other believers for exercise, for meals, for sports programs, and for fun and fellowship.

The church I grew up in was downtown in the middle of a large city. We met and gathered at the church for many different reasons and activities. One of my favorite places in our church was the activities building. This building was equipped with ping pong tables, an exercise room, a craft room, a gym, a place to roller skate, an ice cream shop, and even eight bowling lanes. As kids and teenagers, we spent hours in that building in Bible study, involved in sports, and just having fun. I grew up loving my church and enjoying time with other believers. Many years and churches later, I still dearly love the church and God's people.

What about you? Were you in church as a child? Was it a positive experience? Describe your childhood and youth church experiences. If you did not attend, describe any "spiritual" details you remember.

There is one other wonderful New Testament passage that is used to encourage believers to meet together. Check out Hebrews 10:23-25 in the margin. Read this short passage two times, and then consider the following practical questions.

How do your Christian brothers and sisters help you "hold fast" and continue to hope in the Lord?

In what ways do your fellow church members encourage you to grow in your love and in your good deeds?

> "Let us hold fast the confession of our hope without wavering, for He who promised is faithful. And let us consider one another in order to stir up love and good works, not forsaking the assembling of ourselves together, as is the manner of some, but exhorting one another, and so much the more as you see the Day approaching."
> Hebrews 10:23-25 (NKJV)

How are you able to encourage other Christians to grow in their love and to hold fast?

Who do you "build up" most in the Lord?

_____

Think about those men and women who have encouraged you in your relationship with Jesus Christ. Who are they? How have they made an impact on your life?

Who encourages you most in your walk with the Lord?

_____

How does this person bless you?

_____

Is there anyone who really "stirs you up" and challenges you in the faith?

_____

If so, how do they do this?

_____

Have you told these folks how much they encourage you?

_____

There are so many friends whom God has used to encourage me and challenge me to grow in the Lord. I have several younger friends who ask me great questions about my faith, about the Bible, and about spiritual things. My own children also remind me to read the Bible and to pray because they know how much they need their mom to be filled up with wisdom and to have the law of kindness on my tongue.

My sweet parents have encouraged me to grow in the Lord and in my relationship with Him. They have been such a testimony to my life of what it means to serve the Lord year after year without losing heart. I am blessed by their training, their testimony, and their faithfulness.

However, the person who most encourages me in my walk with the Lord is my husband, Randy. Most of his encouragement comes from the way He models his faith and commitment to Jesus. Every morning, he wakes up early so that he can spend time alone with the Lord. By observing his faithfulness, I am inspired to be faithful in my time alone with God as well.

Close by reading Hebrews 10:23-25 again. Ask the Lord to show you anything He wants to change about your church involvement and your assembling together with other believers. Write down anything that He reveals to you in the coming days...

If you are not a member of a loving, growing fellowship, ask God to lead you to a great church home. Ask Him to give you a church where you can plug in and really experience the joys of getting together with other believers.

Look back over the lesson and choose one verse you can carry with you today.

 Jot down your verse in the margin.

Day Two – Getting Involved with Others by Showing Kindness

....

 Warm-Up and Stretch

Kindness. Compassion. Concern. Caring. These are words that most of us learned in Sunday school, Vacation Bible school, in school, or in our homes. But are these words that we hear as adults? Do most people regularly practice kindness with others?

> "But set an example for the believers in speech, in life, in love, in faith and in purity." 1 Timothy 4:12-13 (NIV)

Chapter 7 heading in margin

As a child, I learned Ephesians 4:32. Maybe you know it? "*Be ye kind one to another, tenderhearted, forgiving one another, even as God for Christ's sake hath forgiven you.*" (KJV)

> "A hothead starts fights; a cool-tempered person tries to stop them."
> Proverbs 15:18 (NLT)

On paper, these words sound pretty easy to understand and follow. But in the real world, it's very hard to be kind and tenderhearted and forgiving. When we get involved with other people, even Christian people, our kindness meters are often stretched and pushed to the limit.

How's your kindness meter? Are you filled with compassion and forgiveness?

When someone steals my parking spot in the Wal-Mart or Target parking lot, I typically...

a. Yell at them & sometimes make "gestures" at them.

b. Say something tacky - under my breath.

c. Think terrible thoughts, but don't speak out loud.

d. Take a deep breath and try to let it go.

e. Other _____.

When someone else gets the praise, the reward, or the promotion I thought I deserved, I typically...

a. Sulk and withdraw my affections from that person altogether.

b. Make sarcastic comments questioning the other person.

c. Get extremely angry and let everyone know.

d. Take it to the Lord and pour out my hurts to Him.

e. Other _____.

If a teacher or coach treats my child in an unfair manner, I...

a. Go see that coach or teacher and let him have it.

b. Talk about the teacher/coach to all of my friends and relatives.

c. Dwell on it, think about it, and let it really get to me.

d. Wait until I calm down, and then see what I can do to help the situation.

e. Take a deep breath, ask for God's help, and try to let it go.

f. Other _____.

When my husband is late again or forgets something important, I...

a. Yell at him and let him have it when he comes in.

b. Use sarcasm and make him pay for it all night long.

c. Use the silent treatment and sulk.

d. Take a deep breath, ask for God's help, and try to let it go.

e. Other _____.

When my best friend leaves me out and chooses to spend time with another friend, I...

a. Yell at her and let her have it when I see her again.

b. Use sarcasm and make her pay for her decision to leave me out.

c. Think terrible thoughts, but don't speak out loud.

d. Give her the cold shoulder and play "games" with her to get her to apologize.

e. Pray and give her the freedom to have other friends while I meet other friends as well.

f. Other _____.

So, how "kind" would you say you are? Are you quick to forgive or do you hold a grudge? Are you the type of person who screams or sulks?

Let's look today at some of the things that the Bible teaches about relationships and about kindness.

 Exercise Your Spiritual Muscles

Start your exercising today by looking to one of the most beloved and famous passages in Scripture. Read this familiar story found in Luke 10:25-37. Then answer the questions below:

Why do you suppose that neither the priest nor the Levite stopped to help the hurting man in the story?

_____

_____

Why did the Samaritan stop to help?

_____

_____

> The Samaritan was most likely just as busy as the other two men, but he took time out of his day to show love and kindness to someone else.

Have you ever noticed that some people are always in a hurry? They have places to go, people to see, and important things to do. The priest and the Levite in this parable were incredibly busy people; they seemed to have no mercy or concern for this poor man who was lying on the side of the road.

The Good Samaritan, however, noticed this hurting man, and took pity on him. The Samaritan was most likely just as busy as the other two men, but he took time out of his day to show love and kindness to someone else.

Think about your typical days. Are you more likely to hurry past people like the priest and Levite? Or, are you alert to the needs of those around you? Explain your answer below.

_____

_____

Years ago when I was driving to the Dallas airport to fly home for a college break, a huge thunderstorm struck. You literally could not see the cars or even the red brake lights in front of you. I pulled over to the side of the interstate to wait for the storm to clear. However, the rain only increased. I knew that I would miss my flight if I didn't at least try to keep driving, but the rain seemed to just grow worse as the minutes ticked by.

After a few moments, a car pulled up in front of me on the side of the road, and a man came running to my car window. He was getting soaked as he offered to lead me toward the airport. I followed him all the way to the airport exit, grateful to have a guide leading the way. I never saw the man again; my mother thinks he may have been an angel unaware. But, I just was grateful for a "Good Samaritan" on a dark and rainy day. More than likely, I would have missed my flight if he hadn't stopped to help.

Look back over the story of the Good Samaritan (Luke 10:25-37) once more.

What do you appreciate about the Samaritan in the Bible story?

_____

_____

Describe how God has used a "Good Samaritan" in your life?

_____

_____

What can you do today to be a "Good Samaritan" to a friend or family member?

_____

_____

Let's look now at a couple of great verses that instruct us in the Bible's ways of kindness. Read each of these verses, and then write down what you find about kindness and compassion.

Philippians 2:2-4 -

_____

_____

Colossians 3:12-14 -

_____

_____

> Dealing with people can be just plain hard, but it is not impossible to live in love and understanding.

Both of these passages challenge us to think more about others than we do about ourselves. Relating to others in love and kindness is never easy. Dealing with people can be just plain hard, but it is not impossible to live in love and understanding. When we act unselfishly and in humility, we are acting like our Savior. Putting our personal interests aside demonstrates the love of Jesus to those around us.

Scripture encourages us to "put on" qualities like compassion and gentleness and patience. We are challenged to bear with others, forgive each other, and to live in unity. Beyond all things, the Bible exhorts us to put on love.

When I think of this act of "putting on" something, I am reminded of my son Riley. A few years ago, Riley had a funny habit that made us all smile. As he would walk through the door from school or any other event, he liked to change his clothes and get comfortable. He would go to his room and put on his big, comfy robe. Riley adored this robe, and he enjoyed taking off his school or church clothes so that he could "put on" his warm and soft robe. He felt safe and comfortable when he would put on this robe. As believers, we would do well to develop the habit of "putting on" the robe of love and kindness.

Those around us would benefit greatly if we regularly put on forgiveness, compassion, and patience.

What kind of "robe" are you putting on most of the time? When you put on your "robe," describe the positive impact on your relationships.

_____

_____

Ask God to make you a vessel of love today. Invite Him to use you to be a "Good Samaritan" to someone in your sphere of influence.

As you get up and go today, keep in mind the words to the old Coca-Cola commercial:

> "What the world needs now is love, sweet love.
> It's the only thing that there's just too little of.
> What the world needs now is love, sweet love.
> No not just for one, but for everyone." Song written by Burt Bacharach.

Consider a verse that you can carry with you today.

 Jot down your verse in the margin.

> "What the world needs now is love, sweet love. It's the only thing that there's just too little of. What the world needs now is love, sweet love. No not just for one, but for everyone." Song written by Burt Bacharach.

Day Three – Getting Involved with Others Through Reaching Out

 Warm-Up and Stretch

If God does care for other people through us, then we have an awesome opportunity to be used by our heavenly Father. We can be His hands of kindness, and His touches of love, His hugs, and His compassionate words and deeds.

> **We can be His hands of kindness, and His touches of love, His hugs, and His compassionate words and deeds.**

We can be Christians who witness with our lives and with our actions. It's not just important to share the Gospel of Christ, but to live it out in front of those around us.

Pray this Scripture today as you begin, *"Father, help me to encourage those who are timid. Take tender care of those who are weak. Be patient with everyone." 1 Thessalonians 5:14 (NLT)*

Think for a minute about those who are in your world.

- How many non-believers do you encounter each day? _____

- How many non-believers do you encounter each week? _____

- How many neighbors do you have that you could love to Jesus? _____

- How many relatives do you know that need the Lord? _____

- How many co-workers do you know with whom you could share the Gospel? _____

- Are there some people with whom you exercise, play golf, or know who need to meet the Lord?

  _____

- Are there people on your bus? In your carpool? On the plane with you? In the meetings with you?

  _____

There are so many people around us every single day who need to hear, see, and experience the Jesus in us. Sometimes we don't even get to say a word, but our lives can be such a witness! That's what we will think about today: How can we witness with our lives?

 Exercise Your Spiritual Muscles

One of my goals is to look for ways each day to just practice little random acts of kindness and to demonstrate God's love. When I can stop and let someone walk in front of my car at the store, I try to do so. When I can open the door for an older person or a mother with a stroller, I try to do this. When I can let someone else get the best parking space, I try to give it to them. My prayer is that my small acts of unselfishness might "shock" them and get their attention.

There's a wonderful verse in <u>Romans 2:4</u> that states, *"God's kindness is intended to lead you to repentance."* (HCSB) My prayer is that I will be a vessel of that kindness that leads to repentance.

How do you suppose God's kindness might lead to someone repenting and trusting Jesus as Lord and Savior?

_____

_____

_____

_____

How can we be God's vessels of kindness to a lost world?

_____

_____

As we show kindness in a cruel and cold world, other people take notice. They observe our actions and our reactions. They notice whether we get upset in traffic, at the cash register, and in the face of challenges. Our neighbors and co-workers are watching to see if our faith makes us better, stronger, and more loving. What do they see when they look at our lives? Do they notice anything different about us?

Think for a moment about your life and the way you interact with those around you. Look at the list below, and check off each kind action that you have taken with an unbeliever:

- I've taken cookies or brownies to a neighbor.
- I've watched one of my neighbor's children.
- I've invited a lost neighbor or friend to church.
- I've made dinner for a friend or neighbor.
- I've taken a co-worker to lunch to get to know them.
- I've had a co-worker into my home for dinner.
- I've been kind to a waiter or waitress that was struggling.
- I've given up my seat or parking spot for a stranger.

Do you think these acts of kindness really matter? Why or why not?

_____

_____

Let's look at what the Bible says about loving the world and being a bright light for our God. Look at each of these verses and make a note of what you learn about loving others for the Kingdom.

Verses	What did you learn about sharing God's love?
Matthew 5:13-16	
1 Timothy 4:12	
1 Peter 2:11-12 and 3:1-3	

Do you like a little salt on your popcorn or corn on the cob? Most of us like some flavoring added to our foods. And, as believers, we have the privilege of being "flavoring" to those around us. What sort of flavor do most of us add? Are we making things taste better to the lost world around us? As we relate to our spouses, our kids, our friends, our co-workers, and those people with whom we come into contact on a regular basis, does our "flavor" draw them closer or do we push them away?

Think about your "flavoring" for a moment. It may not be salty. It may be more of a sweet spice, but your life gives off some sort of flavor. What sort of flavor do you think you are sharing with those around you? Why do you think this?

Let's conclude by making this lesson practical. Use the chart below to help you to do some brainstorming. Try to come up with some ideas that you will actually try!

People I know who need Christ	Two practical ways I can reach out to them and begin to share the love of Jesus

Pray and ask God to give you the courage to actually get out there and try some of these ideas. Begin to reach out to your neighbors and co-workers in some very practical ways. Start small and build a relationship with them. Invite God to use your life to demonstrate His love to those around you.

Look back over today's lesson and find one verse that really stands out to you.

 Jot down your verse in the margin.

Day Four– Getting Involved with Others with a Testimony

....

 Warm-Up and Stretch

Ask God to speak to you today as you study. Use this verse as your prayer, " *In your great love revive me so I can alertly obey your every word. What you say goes, God, and stays, as permanent as the heavens. Your truth never goes out of fashion; it's as up-to-date as the earth when the sun comes up." Psalm 119:88-90 (MSG)*

> "For as long as I shall live, I will testify to love."
> **Words from Avalon song –** "Testify to Love"

Think about the words from this contemporary Christian song.

Then answer the questions aloud as you begin:

- What does most of your life testify?
- Do you testify to the love of God?
- Are you a positive witness by the way you talk, live, spend your money, and such?

Let's begin with prayer as we launch into today's lesson. Why not pray these words, *"Lord, help me to proclaim that Jesus is the Son of God and that He lives in me. I also live in Him. I know how much You love me, and I have put my trust in You." paraphrased from 1 John 4:13-16 (NLT)*

Try the following quiz to better see to what your life testifies. If a poll were taken of your family members, friends, co-workers, what answers would they give to the following questions?

Her life is all about…

    a. Herself   b. Her family

    c. Her job   d. Her hobbies

    e. Her faith in Jesus

She is basically into…

    a. Nice things   b. Travel
    c. Scrap booking   d. Sports
    e. People

Her biggest interests are related to…

    a. Her family   b. Her faith
    c. Her friends   d. Her job
    e. Herself

Her life really testifies to…

_____

_____

_____

 Exercise Your Spiritual Muscles

Let's begin with a few warm-up questions for you to answer:

Have you ever shared your faith with anyone else? If so, who was it?

_____

_____

> **If you were asked to share your "testimony" about your relationship with Jesus, would you know what to share?**

If you were asked to share your "testimony" about your relationship with Jesus, would you know what to share?

If a friend or a neighbor were to ask you about your faith or your "religion," what would you say?

_____

_____

Before this lesson is over, you will have the chance to think through and write out your testimony.

But first, let's look at a great example of a personal testimony in the Bible. Turn to and read <u>1 Timothy 1:12-17</u>. Then answer the following questions:

Who is giving a testimony in these verses?

_____

What is the main message of this testimony?

_____

_____

What do you learn from this person's testimony?

_____

_____

What have you gained from reading this testimony that will help you to write your own testimony?

_____

_____

Now that you've read Paul's testimony about the way God's mercy had changed his life, you are ready to write your own testimony. Even if you have tried this before, I encourage you to go ahead and complete this exercise. Refer back to <u>1 Timothy 1:12-17</u> for additional ideas as you need them.

217

Different Parts of a Testimony	YOUR Personal Testimony
My life before I met Jesus Christ was... (Share in general terms. You do NOT have to give all of the details of your life before Christ.)	
Then, something amazing happened, and I found out how I could have a personal relationship with Jesus. Here's how it happened...	
I prayed and invited Jesus into my heart with a simple prayer. I prayed something like...	
Now, I have a relationship with Him that is real. I am so thankful to know a God who...	

That's it! You've completed your testimony. Why not take the time to write it out in your own words in the space below, or you may want to type it on the computer and print out a copy. After writing or typing it out, read it aloud to someone else—a trusted friend, co-worker, neighbor, or spouse. Invite them to give you some feedback after you share your testimony.

As you close your time today with the Lord, ask God to give you the chance to share your personal testimony with one other person who really needs to hear what God has done in your life. Tell God that you are willing to step out in faith by sharing your story with at least one other person today.

Look back over today's lesson and choose one verse that you will take with you today.

 Jot down your verse in the margin.

Day Five – Getting Involved with Others Through Mentoring

....

 Warm-Up and Stretch

This is it! This is our last exercise session together! It's been an incredible accomplishment for you to make it through this entire study. My prayer is that you have learned, grown closer to Jesus, and gotten in the habit of spending daily time with Him.

As we conclude today, there is a challenge I'd like to issue to you: Don't let this be the end of your spiritual journey! Instead, make this study a beginning for you. Let this day be the day that you determine to continue to move forward and to grow in the Lord. Ask your heavenly Father to speak to your heart and to prepare you to move out of your comfort zone beginning today.

> **Ask your heavenly Father to speak to your heart and to prepare you to move out of your comfort zone beginning today.**

Pray using these verses, *"I will never forget Your precepts, For by them You have given me life. I am Yours, save me; For I have sought Your precepts." Psalm 119:93-94 (NKJV)*

 Exercise Your Spiritual Muscles

Our meeting took place at a local coffee shop. I sat around the table with a few close friends at the conclusion of our yearly Bible study class. A challenge was issued that night to start praying about getting intentionally involved in the lives of some other, younger Christian women. We encouraged each other to pray for at least one younger woman to pour our lives into and to minister to.

I left the meeting thinking of that challenge and of two young women that I wanted to mentor. I began to pray for them and to ask God to send them across my path if He desired for me to mentor them.

Within two weeks, both of those women had come to me and asked if I would mentor them! I did not have to go to them or initiate it in any way. I just asked God to send them my way. He did!

For several months now, I have been meeting these girls for coffee or lunch, having them into my home, and visiting with them at church. Sometimes we pray together, sometimes we share our hearts, and sometimes we talk about the things God is teaching us. These mentoring relationships have become one of the greatest endeavors I have undertaken in quite a great while.

So what about you? Are you investing in the life of someone right now? Are you intentionally mentoring, discipling, or training someone else?

Just off the cuff, if you had to list 3-4 people you could pray about mentoring, who might you list...

_____   _____

_____   _____

How might you go about starting a mentoring relationship with one or more of the folks that you listed?

_____

_____

What sorts of things would you like to do, teach, or study with one of more of these people?

So, what's keeping you from this endeavor?

_____

Let's look at a wonderful passage about mentoring that's found in the New Testament. These verses are printed below.

<u>Duties of the Older and Younger</u>

"But as for you, speak the things which are fitting for sound doctrine. Older men are to be temperate, dignified, sensible, sound in faith, in love, in perseverance. Older women likewise are to be reverent in their behavior, not malicious gossips, nor enslaved to much wine, teaching what is good, that they may encourage the young women to love their husbands, to love their children, to be sensible, pure, workers at home, kind, being subject to their own husbands, that the word of God may not be dishonored." Titus 2:1-5 (NASB)

Look back at the verses taken from Titus 2. Then, answer the following questions:

Why do you think the Bible encourages those who are older in age and in spiritual maturity to encourage those who are younger in age or in "the Faith"?

_____

_____

_____

_____

_____

According to Titus, what are some ways that we can encourage those who are "younger" than we are?

_____

_____

> **Why not let God use you to positively influence someone else for His Kingdom?**

Personally, I am so grateful for those older women and men who invested in my life and mentored me. Most likely you also had men and women who trained you and taught you just as the Titus passage mentions. To be encouraged to love our spouses and children, to be sensible people, to take care of our homes, to submit to our husbands, and to honor the Word of God; these are all wonderful and valuable lessons that we can pass along to younger women.

Close your time today by asking God to make you a willing, wise mentor in someone else's life. You may only be 18 or be pushing 80. God can use you if you are willing to be used. Age is not really a factor in God's economy. Stage of life is not a factor either. He is looking for some available men and women—some believers who want to make an impact in the lives of the people around them.

Why not let God use you to positively influence someone else for His Kingdom?

Glance back over this lesson one more time. Find a great verse or idea and take it with you.

 Jot down your verse in the margin.

"What I do you cannot do; but what you do, I cannot do. The needs are great, and none of us, including me, ever do great things. But we can all do small things, with great love, and together we can do something wonderful." Mother Teresa

Exercise tips of the week

~ God can use you if you're willing to be used!

~ Kindness opens many doors into people's lives.

~ A phone call, a card, or a plate of brownies are all great witnessing tools!

Reviewing what we've learned

First... Get involved in a Bible-believing, God-honoring, friendly and growing church.	**Second...** Start reaching out to others with acts of kindness and compassion. Do for others what you'd love for them to do for you.
Third... Try to cultivate at least one relationship with an unbeliever. Reach out in kindness to this person.	**Last...** Ask God to give you one other person who you can mentor and pour your life into. If you've never been mentored, ask Him to give you a wise friend.

Prayer of Closing Commitment

Lord, I desire to live my life unselfishly for You.

I want to spend time each day alone with You in prayer and Bible study. Give me a heart and a passion for Your Word.

I desire to memorize Your Word and to carry it with me throughout the day. Help me to do this.

I want to listen to You and hear from heaven. Make me more sensitive to Your Holy Spirit. Give me eyes to see You at work and to hear You when You speak.

I desire to set my mind only on good things. Keep evil, unnecessary, and harmful things away from me. Give me wisdom in my reading, what I watch, in my conversations, and in my life.

I desire to get involved in the lives of others—both believers and nonbelievers. I ask You to fill my life with godly people who will encourage me to be more like You.

Also, give me the chance to impact the lives of others. I ask for some younger person that I can mentor and encourage to be more like Jesus.

Thank you for teaching me and loving me.

I love you, Lord.

Special Thanks To:

My wonderful Bible study group at Englewood Baptist Church who first tried this study with me – for your encouragement, feedback, ideas, support and love:

- Margie Adams
- Pam Barnes
- Nina Blevins
- Barbara Boone
- Judy Carroll
- Nancy French
- Joan Goarck
- Phyllis Hardy
- Morgan Haskins
- Melanie Hicks
- Ruby Hobbs
- Mazie Holloman
- Sandra Johnson
- Angie Lane
- Donna Long
- Jeanette Mallory
- Mary Ellen Marshall
- Earlene McGinnis
- Rosanne Mascarenhas
- Betty Michal
- Evelyn Murray
- Donna Patterson
- Delia Perry
- Tami Pridgen
- Robin Powell
- Laura Ramsey
- Monica Sanchez
- Sally Sandifer
- Shan Stocks
- Sandra Thompson
- Beverly Weigle

**Those friends who helped with editing, ideas,
and hours of looking over this material:**

Becky Abel   Tammy Benfield   Phyllis Hardy
Debbie Wheeler   Randy Redd   Jim Gillentine

**Those friends who prayed, generously supported, and
encouraged me to go forward with this project:**

Jo Anna & Larry Gurley

My sweet family for all of their encouragement:

Randy, Riley, & Emily
Vernon & Elsie Redd
Roland & Sarah Maddox

"I thank my God always concerning you for the grace of God which was given to you by Christ Jesus." 1 Corinthians 1:4 (NKJV)

Reference Page

* Quotes in many of the text boxes taken from the book 14,000 Quips and Quotes, E.C. McKenzie, Hendrickson Publishers, 1980. Permission granted in writing for quotes as long as word count stayed below a certain number.

Specific References:

1] *Page 7 – "God is Watching Over You" song by Phil Joel. Released June 27, 2000 by Sparrow Records.*

2] *Page 30 - Definition paraphrased from E-Sword Bible freeware, 2000-2009*

3] *Page 31 - Definition paraphrased from E-Sword Bible freeware, 2000-2009*

4] *Page 33 – Quote by Dr. Adrian Rogers – shared from the pulpit at Bellevue Baptist Church on numerous occasions. Shared by permission of his wife, Joyce Rogers.*

5] *Page 34 - Definition paraphrased from E-Sword Bible freeware, 2000-2009*

6] *Page 35 - Definition paraphrased from E-Sword Bible freeware, 2000-2009*

7] *Page 37 - Definition paraphrased from E-Sword Bible freeware, 2000-2009*

8] *Page 38 - Definition paraphrased from E-Sword Bible freeware, 2000-2009*

9] *Page 39 - Definition paraphrased from E-Sword Bible freeware, 2000-2009*

10] *Page 40 - Definition paraphrased from E-Sword Bible freeware, 2000-2009*

11] *Page 40 - Definition paraphrased from E-Sword Bible freeware, 2000-2009*

12] *Page 63 – Poem "God in the Morning" from website* www.biblereadingschedule.com

13] *Page 67 – Quote by Adrian Rogers shared in a sermon at Bellevue Baptist Church. Shared by permission of his wife, Joyce Rogers.*

14] *Page 82 – Story adapted from book* Codependent No More *by Melody Beattie, Hazelton Books, September 1, 1992.*

15] *Page 86 – Prayer examples taken from* A Mother's Garden of Prayer *by Sarah Maddox & Patti Webb, B & H Publishing Group, 2001.*

16] *Page 97 – Story shared by Jennifer Walker with permission.*

17] *Page 119 – Idea original with Brother Bob Sorrell. Shared with permission.*

18] *Page 134 – Idea of 60/60 found in "Leadership" magazine, John Burke, Spring 2009, Pages 26-29.*

19] *Page 143 – Idea shared by Dr. Adrian Rogers. Don't know if it was original with him.*

20] *Page 147 – AWANAS Clubs International. On the web:* www.awana.org.

21] *Page 151 –* Celebration of Discipline *by Richard Foster, Harper San Francisco, October 5, 1988.*

22] *Page 157– "Cry out to Jesus" song by Third Day. Released September 13, 2005 by Essential Records.*

23] *Page 170 – The "God Watch" idea was shared years ago in "Discipleship Journal" magazine. Year and edition unknown. DJ is published by NavPress and can be found at:* www.navpress.com.

24] *Page 171–* <u>Experiencing God</u> *by Henry Blackaby, B & H Books, September 1, 2008.*

25] *Page 182 – Debbie Settle's ideas about "Monuments to God's Faithfulness" were shared at a retreat with First Baptist Church of Snellville, GA. Used with permission.*

About the Author...

MELANIE REDD

Melanie's passion is to help men and women to literally step closer to Jesus. She holds a degree in Education from Baylor University, has spent her adult years teaching in the school and church classroom. She currently serves as the Director of Women's Ministry at Faith Baptist Church, teaches women's classes at Mid-America Baptist Theological Seminary, and homeschools her two teenagers. Melanie is married to Randy, and the family makes their home in Memphis, TN.

Melanie would love to get your feedback or to hear from you. You can reach her by email at steppingcloser@gmail.com, on the web at www.melanieredd. blogspot.com, and on Twitter at www.twitter.com/MelanieRedd.

LaVergne, TN USA
18 August 2010
193741LV00004B/2/P